31549
5/07

DATE DUE

OCT 3 1 2008		
FEB 0 5 2013		

Demco

BIOHAZARDS

SCIENCE & TECHNOLOGY IN FOCUS

BIOHAZARDS

Humanity's Battle
with Infectious Disease

Sean M. Grady
and
John Tabak, Ph.D.

☑️ Facts On File
An imprint of Infobase Publishing

BIOHAZARDS: Humanity's Battle with Infectious Disease

Facts On File, Inc.
An imprint of Infobase Publishing
132 West 31st Street
New York NY 10001

Library of Congress Cataloging-in-Publication Data

Grady, Sean M., 1965–
Biohazards: humanity's battle with infectious disease /
Sean M. Grady and John Tabak.
p. cm.—(Science & technology in focus)
ISBN 0-8160-4687-5
1. Communicable diseases. 2. Medical microbiology. 3. Bioterrorism.
4. Epidemiology. I. Tabak, John. II. Title. III. Series.
RA643.G734 2006
614.5'99—dc22   2005005610

Facts On File books are available at special discounts when purchased in bulk quantities for businesses, associations, institutions, or sales promotions. Please call our Special Sales Department in New York at (212) 967-8800 or (800) 322-8755.

You can find Facts On File on the World Wide Web at http://www.factsonfile.com

Text design by Erika K. Arroyo
Cover design by Nora Wertz
Illustrations by Jeremy Eagle

Printed in the United States of America

MP Hermitage 10 9 8 7 6 5 4 3 2 1

This book is printed on acid-free paper.

CONTENTS

PART 2: BIOHAZARDS THROUGHOUT HISTORY

PART 3: MODERN-DAY RISKS

ACKNOWLEDGMENTS

John Tabak wishes to thank Frank K. Darmstadt, executive editor, for his help with this project, and Amy L. Conver, for her excellent copyediting of the manuscript. Special thanks to Penelope Pillsbury and the staff of the Brownell Library, Essex Junction, Vermont, for their assistance with the many questions that arose during the preparation of this book.

INTRODUCTION

We live in a sea of microorganisms. They grow around us, upon us, and inside us. Most are benign, some are helpful, and a very small percentage of them are dangerous. But the harmful microorganisms can be extremely dangerous. They are responsible for many millions of deaths each year. The most potentially dangerous of these disease-causing organisms, or *pathogens*, are called *biohazards*.

Microorganisms occupy microenvironments, where the length of a generation is often measured in minutes or hours rather than years. Short generational times enable colonies of these organisms to grow with astonishing speed. Too small to move far on their own, many pathogens have adapted to live inside rats, birds, mosquitoes, and other *vectors*—creatures that transmit pathogens from one host to another—and so they are able to travel from city to city and nation to nation as easily as their hosts, where they sometimes leave their nonhuman hosts to infect new human populations.

Despite the very important role that pathogens play in the lives of individuals and the history of nations, scientists have only been aware of the existence of microorganisms for a few centuries; they became aware of the dangers posed by pathogens less than 150 years ago. The earliest so-called miracle drugs, substances capable of destroying infectious organisms without harming their human host, were discovered in the first half of the 20th century. The revelation that microorganisms can adapt to these drugs and flourish in spite of them was first recognized in the latter half of the 20th century. The more we learn, the more complex the situation appears.

This book describes some of history's most dangerous germs as well as their structure, ecology, and the symptoms with which they are commonly associated. It describes some of the ways these pathogens have affected societies and some of the ways that societies have attempted to counter the pathogens. Finally, this book describes some of the very different ways that scientists and physicians have learned to understand disease-causing microorganisms as they strive to control them.

PART 1

The Lethality
of the Very Small

1

INVISIBLE TO THE HUMAN EYE

It was one of the strangest *epidemics* ever to hit the United States of America.

In May and June 2003, at least 50 people living in Wisconsin, Indiana, Illinois, and New Jersey came down with an infection that caused large pustules—pus-filled blisters—to spread over their bodies, accompanied by fevers, chills, and large rashes. At first, none of these patients' physicians knew what the disease was. The symptoms were similar to those of chickenpox, but the pustules were too large, and many of the patients either had contracted chickenpox already or had received a *vaccine* against it.

Public health officials worried that the outbreak of the disease in the Midwest might be the first sign of an attack by terrorists using smallpox, a deadly disease that was all but eradicated in the 20th century. The threat of *bioterrorism* was and is very real: In 2001, 22 people came down with, and five died from, a disease called *anthrax*, after an unknown terrorist sent a handful of anthrax-bearing letters to politicians, journalists, and other citizens along the East Coast. Terrorists, however, were not responsible for the 2003 epidemic.

In fact, every one of the mysterious infections proved to be monkeypox, a disease caused by a *virus* similar to those that cause smallpox and chickenpox. The problem was that monkeypox was virtually unknown outside the continent of Africa. A few researchers who study *infectious diseases* in the United States had samples of the monkeypox virus, but it was determined that none of these samples had caused the outbreak. And while it is possible for people to come down with the disease if they encounter infected animals (though called monkeypox, the virus also appears in squirrels, mice, porcupines, and other rodents), none of those infected with the virus had ever visited Africa.

In fact, the only factor common to all the infected individuals was that they had recently bought prairie dogs, animals native to the American Southwest, as pets. State health officials and specialists in infectious disease from the federal *Centers for Disease Control and Prevention* (also known as the *CDC*) examined the link between the patients and the prairie dogs. Testing the pets revealed that they carried the virus. "But wait," the scientists said. "How could animals from an American desert become infected with an African virus?"

The path that the virus took from the African wilds to the American pet owners was a complicated one. A pet distributor near Chicago, Illinois, who specialized in rodents, had received a Gambian giant pouched rat that had been imported from West Africa. The rat was infected with the poxvirus, a fact that the importers did not know. While in the distributor's shop, the virus infected the distributor's stock of prairie dogs. Another distributor in Milwaukee, Wisconsin, bought the rat and some of the prairie dogs from the Illinois distributor, selling the prairie dogs to a couple of pet shops and at a pet show. The people who bought the animals as pets, as well as some of the people who sold them, were the ones who came down with monkeypox.

In contrast to some other, more famous epidemics, the monkeypox incident was not especially serious. Although federal officials announced that as many as 115 people may have been exposed to the disease, they also pointed out that no one seemed to be catching it directly from other people. Only direct contact with a sick rodent seemed to transmit the virus. Better still, no one died of the disease: Seven people received hospital treatment, and the others were *quarantined* at home until the disease ran its course. In an effort to prevent additional outbreaks, the CDC and the U.S. Food and Drug Administration, which oversee the importation of animals to the United States, banned the importation, transportation, and sale of six types of African rodents, including the Gambian rat.

functioning of the body as they feed and reproduce within the cells and organs of their hosts.

Molds live on dead plant or animal tissues and reproduce via *spores*. Like other fungi, such as mushrooms, molds can be beneficial (the first *antibiotic* drugs came from molds) or poisonous, producing toxic chemicals that can sicken or kill. In many forms of mold-caused illnesses, it is the mold's spores that cause problems rather than the mold itself.

Occasionally, mold-caused diseases become the subject of intensive news coverage. In the late 1990s and early 2000s, people across the United States claimed to have been sickened by outbreaks of so-called toxic mold in buildings. People either abandoned their homes or spent thousands of dollars eliminating mold from crawl spaces, basements, attics, and other areas where the mold was growing. Some school districts shut down classrooms or entire schools in which mold was detected; other public buildings suffered similar fates. Precisely how toxic much of this mold is, however, remains an open question.

The Most Virulent Diseases

Fortunately for people, animals, and plants, most microbes on Earth are harmless. Only a few of them are *pathogenic*, or able to cause disease, and then only if they are able to enter certain areas of the body. For instance, while billions of streptococcus and staphylococcus bacteria may live on a person's skin, they rarely do more than cause pimples or boils. If they enter the throat or find their way below the skin—through a cut or a puncture—they can develop quite rapidly into severe, even life-threatening, infections that require powerful antibiotics to treat.

The most deadly diseases often are those that people rarely contract. *Hemorrhagic fevers*, diseases whose symptoms include large amounts bleeding, are some of the most virulent of all diseases. The limited spread of many of these diseases, which include Ebola, is not due to advanced medical knowledge. There are no cures for many of these illnesses, nor are there vaccines available to ward off the viruses. Quite simply, hemorrhagic fevers often kill their victims too quickly for outbreaks to spread very far.

Of greater concern are diseases that progress more slowly but can spread to a larger population. Tuberculosis is a slow-acting infection that damages the lungs and other organs, causing extreme fatigue and

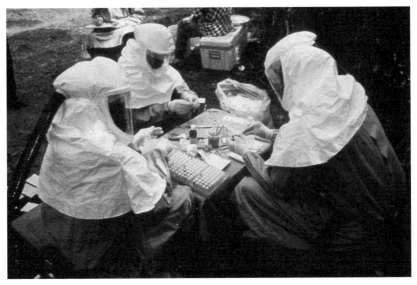

CDC and Zairean scientists take samples of animals during a 1995 Ebola epidemic. It is believed that the Ebola virus's "natural reservoir" is an African animal.
[Courtesy of Dr. Fred Murphy, Centers for Disease Control and Prevention]

a lingering, wasting death. Left untreated, tuberculosis patients can spread the bacteria that cause the disease by coughing the microbes into the air. Prisoners, for example, and anyone else who lives in crowded, poorly ventilated conditions are at risk of contracting tuberculosis and spreading it. Tuberculosis kills approximately 2 million people each year, in part because the disease is easy to transmit and those with the disease remain active for a long period of time, during which the disease is transmissible.

In a way, it is more difficult to stop a disease like tuberculosis than it is to deal with fast-acting diseases. A microbe with a long incubation period—the time from when the microbe enters a person to the onset of symptoms—can spread to more people than one that can strike down its victims within a few hours. The longer one remains infectious, the better the microbe's chances of transmission to a new host.

Although most microbes pose no immediate risk, the longer-term risks are more difficult to evaluate. Microbes change, and as they change, the symptoms that they cause and the hosts that they are able to infect change as well. Health experts fully expect to see new and possibly dangerous diseases evolve over time. Some of the microbes responsible for these diseases are sure to be descendants of microbes that pose no risk to us at present. The evolution of new and potentially dangerous microbes is a fact of life. The challenge is to adapt as fast as the microbes and to develop strategies and technologies that will protect the public health as fast as the new challenges arise.

2

WHERE THE
SMALL THINGS ARE

Despite their small size, microbes exhibit some of the same behaviors as their more complex multicellular counterparts. Of special importance to those interested in biohazards are the reproductive behaviors of microbes. Given the right conditions—adequate food and a safe environment—many microbes are able to increase their numbers at an astonishing rate. Because disease microbes reproduce inside living creatures, the host becomes ill.

Many disease microbes developed their parasitic ways thousands, if not millions, of years ago. Paleontologists—scientists who study fossil bones—have discovered evidence of dental infection from as far back as the age of dinosaurs. Mummies thousands of years old have borne the signs of maladies such as skin infections, *syphilis* (a sexually transmitted disease), and sinus trouble. And documents from ancient Egypt, China, Greece, and the Roman Empire describe outbreaks of smallpox, malaria, and other maladies, some of which have in recent years been brought under control.

Other microbes are newcomers to the world of infectious disease. Diseases in this category include Ebola, which causes death through uncontrollable bleeding and the destruction of internal organs,

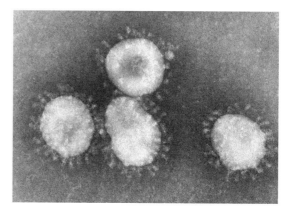

Coronavirus. Viruses in this class are characterized by a crown-like (corona) appearance when viewed under high magnification. For example, a type of coronavirus caused severe acute respiratory syndrome (SARS). [Courtesy of Dr. Fred Murphy, Centers for Disease Control and Prevention]

HIV/AIDS, which attacks the immune system and leaves its victims vulnerable to other diseases, and *severe acute respiratory syndrome* (*SARS*), which is a dangerous flu-like disease that first appeared in 2003. Some of these new diseases seem to have originated in animals and only recently developed into forms that can infect human beings. Over time, the viruses that cause these diseases may evolve into forms that are less lethal to human life. There is ample evidence that this can occur; it benefits neither party when a microorganism destroys the host upon which its survival depends.

The Opportunistic Evolution of Disease

Microorganisms, hazardous and benign, evolved as part of an ecological system that is nearly as old as Earth itself. Billions of years ago, all life on Earth was unicellular. Each organism was an autonomous, microscopic creature with its own complement of genes embedded in cytoplasm and protected from the surrounding environment by a cell wall. Presumably, each single-celled organism competed with other single-celled organisms to survive. There are, however, advantages to cooperation as well as individual competition, and some cells evolved the ability to grow together. These multicellular structures were simple at first, but over time the component cells became specialized and highly interdependent. Multicellular creatures, plant and animal, evolved from their unicellular ancestors.

As more sophisticated multicellular animal and plant life developed, some microbes evolved the ability to live within the bodies of the larger organisms. Biologically, this was a very efficient way to survive. Rather than risk life in direct contact with the forces of nature, microbes could feed and reproduce in the relative safety of an enclosed environment. Animal or plant cells were rich sources of nutrients, as was the food the animals and plants ingested. The larger and more complex the plant or animal, the greater the opportunity for the microbes to find a home.

Over the course of many millions of years, microorganisms evolved together with their multicellular hosts. The genetic code of the microbes, like that of their hosts, changed from one generation to the next. The changes may have been the result of mutations, which are random changes in a microbe's genetic code, or they may have resulted from the direct exchange of genetic material between microbes or between the microbe and the host. Changes also resulted from *selection pressures*. Such changes occur in gene frequencies from one generation to the next and result from the fact that variations in the genetic inheritance of individuals affect the rate at which they are able to produce viable offspring.

The selection pressures on microbes changed dramatically when humankind began to abandon the practice of living in small groups while following a hunter-gatherer existence. As people domesticated animals, developed agriculture, and settled in their first villages, they changed the patterns of disease transmission by changing the environment in which the germs existed. Bacteria and viruses that once plagued only cattle or swine found their way into other livestock and occasionally into humans with whom they coexisted. Farming also stirred up soil bacteria and mold spores, which farmers inhaled. The changes that humans instituted in their own environment created new environments and new possibilities for the transmission of microbes, and the microbes adapted accordingly.

Deadly Strangers

While multicellular organisms may evolve defense mechanisms to protect themselves from the microbes *endemic* to their environment, they sometimes prove extremely vulnerable to new, unfamiliar pathogens. Microbes may be unfamiliar to their new hosts because they have migrated into the area or because they only recently acquired an adaptation that enabled them to utilize a new species of host. Microbes are generally unable to bridge the distances that separate distant human settlements themselves. They depend, instead, on vectors, organisms that are able to transport and transmit the pathogen from one population to the next. Insects, birds, and mammals have all served as vectors for microbes that prey upon humans.

Often, however, the best vectors are human. As societies developed and people traveled to new areas of the world, they carried pathogens with them and unwittingly introduced these pathogens to the people they encountered during their journeys. Once European nations, especially the Portuguese under the leadership of Henry the Navigator (1394–1460), developed the technology necessary to sail the oceans, there were few places left on Earth that European explorers could not reach.

Chickens in a modern egg farm. Modern farming practices have created new environments for domesticated animals and the microbes that prey on them. [Courtesy of David Fraizer/The Image Works]

The results were often disastrous for the native peoples they encountered. The Europeans, especially the Spanish, Portuguese, English, French, and Dutch, introduced a number of diseases to the lands that they explored and conquered, and the indigenous populations had no immunity to these diseases. Smallpox exacted a terrible toll on the native peoples of North and South America. In general, the mortality rates were much higher among indigenous peoples than among Europeans infected with the same disease. For example, the Massachuset, an Algonquin-speaking people after whom the state of Massachusetts is named, suffered a smallpox epidemic in 1633. Almost the entire tribe died. The same tragedy was repeated again and again throughout the Americas. Smallpox did to the indigenous peoples of North and South America what the *plague* did to Europeans a few centuries before. It is estimated that upward of 50 percent of Native Americans died from diseases introduced by Europeans, and often they died before they had even seen a European.

Even measles, which among Europeans had a comparatively low mortality rate, was a significant source of mortality among many that the Europeans first encountered. Some historians attribute the high rate of mortality to the fact that virtually everyone became ill when one of these diseases was introduced for the first time. (Because no member of the affected population had encountered the disease before, the entire population was simultaneously vulnerable.) As a consequence, there was no one to administer care. Some eyewitness accounts seem to support this view when they describe how some died of the disease and some died of hunger because they were too weak to prepare food for themselves and no one was well enough to help.

The unintended transmission of disease is still a part of life, and in some ways it has actually become easier for diseases to spread. On land, germs can spread as fast as a car can travel on a highway or a high-speed train can roar along the tracks. By air, a sick traveler can carry an exotic virus home in a day or two at most, and even ships, now the slowest mode of travel, remain able to efficiently transport germs from port to port.

A microbe does not, however, have to travel from a distant environment in order to be new to one's immune system. Every year, new forms of the influenza virus run rampant through the bodies of tens of millions of people. Many of these people have had the flu before and have developed antibodies against the virus that caused it, yet they still come down with the disease the following year. If a flu infection causes the body to develop antibodies to the virus that caused it, shouldn't those who were infected previously be immune?

Hong Kong during the SARS epidemic. Note the many masks. [Courtesy of Bill Lai/The Image Works]

The situation is more complicated than it first appears, because the flu virus is not one strain of virus but many strains. Furthermore, the influenza virus is remarkably adept at infecting humans and nonhumans alike. Chickens and pigs, two of the world's most common farm animals, are also vulnerable to influenza. As with many other viruses, influenza viruses sometimes exchange bits of DNA with other organisms, and as they change genetic makeup they sometimes change their infectious properties. This genetic shuffling can create new strains of the virus. Once a new strain comes into being, humanity is once again vulnerable.

The 2003 outbreak of SARS, severe acute respiratory syndrome, is a good example of the problems this gene-swapping, species-jumping ability can create. SARS, a flu-like illness that causes lung infections and other complications, is thought to have originated in a nonhuman host in the People's Republic of China. In rural areas of China, people and animals often live in close enough proximity to provide animal-dwelling microbes with many opportunities to make the transition to a human host. Occasionally, a microbe will succeed. In the case of SARS, a strain of virus developed the ability to make the transition to human beings. Such a jump is rare, but it need only occur once to begin an epidemic, provided the virus can pass from person to person. This is what happened in the case of the SARS epidemic.

Once the SARS virus made the transition from a nonhuman to human host, it began spreading rapidly. Air travelers spread it from southeastern China to Hong Kong, Taiwan, and North America. Cities, such as Toronto, Canada, were stricken with the disease and were unofficially quarantined by airlines and travel companies until the disease was eliminated. Later, cities and regions that were infected celebrated when their health officials declared that they were "SARS-free." Still, the fact that the disease leaped from the China countryside across the Pacific Ocean in such a short time is yet another sign that changes in transportation technology have also introduced new risks to the public health.

Growth and Transmission

It is not uncommon for a sick person to personalize his or her illness—that is, to imagine it as a living, thinking beast that is attacking them from the inside, something that deliberately causes pain and suffering. It is true that most illnesses are caused by organisms that harm their hosts in order to live. But there is no thought behind their activity. A microbe's actions are its response to its environment. If conditions are right for it to grow, it will grow. If not, it will die or remain dormant until conditions improve. This is as true of the most complex multicellular parasites as it is true of the simplest.

Despite the absence of intent on the part of the pathogen, when a vulnerable population—whether human, animal, or plant—comes in contact with a new pathogen, the effects can be devastating. Encountering no resistance, the microbe will grow rapidly in or on its new host, spreading to others through whatever vector is available. People often say that a disease "spreads like wildfire," since the pattern of an epidemic often resembles that of a fire as it travels through a forest or across an open prairie. From one or a handful of initial cases, a disease will travel to family, friends, neighbors, and even strangers who happen to pick up the microbes that cause the illness.

Transmission is accidental: Someone with a head cold may sneeze while walking down a corridor; a minute or two later, someone else will walk down the corridor and inhale some of the viruses that are still floating in the air. A mosquito will draw blood from someone who recently developed malaria and later inject some of the malarial parasites into the bloodstream of its next victim. Someone who becomes sexually intimate with an infected person may contract a sexually transmitted disease. Yet in these and other cases, the microbes will not have chosen their victims. Instead, they are convected passively from host to host in a game of biological "hot potato."

Other factors make the process of disease transmission even more complex. For instance, some people are carriers of some diseases. The microbe that causes the disease may reside in the person without the person demonstrating any symptoms of the disease. Varying levels of immunity to disease reflect variations in one's individual genetic makeup as well as variations in how each individual's immune system, that system of the body whose function is to resist infection, has developed prior to exposure.

One of the best-known cases of a person being immune to the effects of a deadly disease involved a cook named Mary Mallon (ca. 1870–1938). She is best remembered as Typhoid Mary because although she carried the germ that caused the disease, she was immune to its effects.

Typhoid is caused by a bacterium, *Salmonella typhi*, which is transmitted via contaminated food or water. The disease is sometimes fatal. One of the possible symptoms is a perforated intestine, which may result in septicemia (blood poisoning). Other possible complications include heart failure, pneumonia, encephalitis, and *meningitis*. One of the remarkable characteristics of typhoid is that for about 5 percent of those who contract the disease, the bacterium takes up relatively permanent residence in the body. Most of the individuals in this 5 percent will exhibit no symptoms of the disease, but they remain capable of passing the disease to others. They become ideal vectors for typhoid.

Mary Mallon was a healthy-looking carrier of typhoid. She was infamous in her day because she worked as a cook and infected those individuals for whom she prepared food. In fact, even after a typhoid outbreak was traced to her, she insisted on continuing to work as a cook. When confronted by New York City Department of Health engineer George Soper with the fact that she was a typhoid-carrier, she simply disappeared from the public eye and found another job as a cook. She was again discovered working as a cook by Soper. She was eventually quarantined for years, during which time she appealed her detention in the courts. She was eventually released, but when two typhoid epidemics occurred—one in a hospital and one at a sanitorium, both in New Jersey—Soper suspected her involvement. He found her and discovered that she had cooked at both institutions. Mallon was quarantined for 24 more years until her death. Investigators attributed 51 cases, including three deaths, of typhoid directly to Mallon, and a much larger number of cases are indirectly attributed to her. (An indirect case is one in which the typhoid microbe could be traced back to Mallon through third parties.)

Mary Mallon is an extreme example of how some people are better able to tolerate pathogens than others. There is no way to say for sure which man, woman, or child will resist the effects of an infectious microbe and which ones will be sickened or killed. Age, physical condition, and lifestyle can play a role in how well people withstand the assault of an infection. The fact remains, however, that just as there exist variations in the infectious properties of pathogens, there also exist variations in the host's ability to resist their effects.

KEEPING THINGS
UNDER WRAPS

Dealing with infectious diseases is a problem of microbial population control. Human and animal bodies are hostile places for germs, but aside from the immune system's ability to recognize and destroy most foreign organisms that have entered the body, the body's physical and chemical characteristics often kill or remove many microbes before they have a chance to gain a foothold. Even when microbes manage to survive inside the body, they have to multiply many times before they begin to have a harmful effect. It often takes many billions of germs to overwhelm the body's defenses and make their presence felt in the form of symptoms of disease.

Bacteria reproduce with astonishing speed. Most microbes reproduce far more rapidly than do multicellular organisms. Under the right conditions, some bacteria will double their numbers once every 20 minutes. In absolute numbers, this growth rate may not seem fast initially. Beginning with a single bacterium, it would take about two and a half hours for one bacterium to grow into a colony of 100. But in five hours, that single bacterium will have grown into a colony of approximately 16,000 individuals. After eight hours, the population count will be nearly 17 million. Each species of disease microbe reproduces at its own rate, but part of the reason they are successful is that they can reproduce fast enough to outstrip the body's ability to combat them.

The symptoms of disease are not simply related to the number of germs present in the body, however. Some bacteria produce poisonous chemicals as waste products, while others release toxins after they die. Much of the swelling and soreness of a bacterial infection is the body's reaction to these poisons.

Viruses destroy the cells they infect, as floods of newly created microbes burst out of their incubators. Tiny parasitic worms and other microorganisms, such as the protozoa that cause malaria, do the same thing, invading and reproducing inside cells or organs. Most people are unaware of the details of their own immune response, but they can often detect certain indicators of immune system activity, including (depending on the disease) fever and fatigue.

By the time a person notices symptoms of disease, the disease itself is usually well under way. In particular, one can often be contagious—able to spread the disease to other people—before one displays any symptoms. Such a situation is advantageous to the microbes that cause the disease. A colony of microbes will eventually die out unless it can spread to new victims. An active, healthy-looking contagious host is an ideal vector, because he or she offers many opportunities for the microbe to spread from one individual to the next.

The diseases that have survived to plague humanity are exactly the ones that were able to spread from host to host before the parent populations died out. One point of attack for those interested in controlling the spread of a disease is the mechanism by which the organism moves from host to host. Interrupting the life cycle of a microbe by containing it within an already infected population does no good for those already infected, but it is an important line of defense for those not yet infected. The same strategy of containment applies to laboratories where scientists study biohazardous organisms. These researchers have learned to take many precautions when studying disease microbes so that they can contain them in the lab and not transmit them to the uninfected general population.

Levels of Biosafety

Historically, physicians gave little thought to matters of cleanliness. This remained true for decades after the discovery that microbes caused disease. Physicians' offices and apothecary shops (the forerunners of today's pharmacies) were often tidy in the sense that all equipment was put away at the end of the day and all drug ingredients stored in their containers, but equipment wasn't sterilized. They did not even try to sterilize their instruments. Not for lack of technology (they could always have placed the instruments in boiling water); rather, the *idea* of sterility was absent. Even as late as the early years of the 20th century, many physicians went from patient to patient without thoroughly washing or cleaning their instruments; they operated on multiple patients without changing their clothes.

Conditions in laboratories were not much better. They often conducted their studies in the open air of the laboratory workbench, putting themselves at risk of contracting the maladies they were trying to study. Decades after scientists in France and Germany made the connection between microbes and the diseases they cause—most notably microbiologist Louis Pasteur of France and bacteriologist Robert Koch of Germany—many researchers continued to work with extremely hazardous pathogens in conditions that were not much safer than those of a college-level chemistry classroom.

Starting in the 1940s, disease researchers began categorizing each disease organism based mainly on two standards: how dangerous the organism is to human beings and how easy it is for a person to become infected. The researchers began the classification scheme as a step toward establishing safety protocols for those engaged in the study of infectious disease. Over the next few decades, disease-research laboratories and government health agencies developed equipment and lab techniques to make studying the microbes that cause disease safer. This work focused on placing as many barriers as was necessary and practical between researchers and microbes and on setting up procedures for staff to follow to prevent the microbes from escaping the confines of the lab.

This work continued until the early 1980s, when the world health community adopted a system of four *biosafety* levels, or BSLs, that measured each research laboratory's ability to handle progressively more dangerous microbes. In turn, researchers classified the world's microscopic organisms according to the minimum BSL required to handle that organism safely.

Biosafety Level One, or BSL-1, describes a laboratory designed to experiment with microbes that are not likely to pose a threat, either to the public or to the people who handle them in hospitals or laboratories. Most of the body's natural flora—the bacteria that exist on or inside every person and animal on the planet—fall into this category, as do common soil bacteria and other "everyday" microbes. Since these organisms usually do not threaten peoples' lives, any laboratory exposure is generally considered low risk and sophisticated containment procedures are unnecessary. Organisms that cause disease in animals but not in healthy adult humans also may be studied in a BSL-1 laboratory.

Most high school and college chemistry laboratories either operate at BSL-1 already or could easily be brought up to that standard. The only precaution needed at this level is a sink for hand washing, and the only barrier needed between the lab and the outside world is a door.

Biosafety Level Two, or BSL-2, laboratories are designed to handle microbes that cause disease in humans but that can be safely handled with a moderate amount of caution. Viruses such as HIV and hepatitis B and bacteria such as the *Salmonella* that cause some forms of food poisoning, are sometimes called BSL-2 pathogens. Commonly encountered diseases, such as influenza or chicken pox, also are handled at this level. Safety measures in a BSL-2 lab include gowns, gloves, goggles and masks, as well as biosafety cabinets, semi-enclosed workspaces that shield lab workers from accidental splashes. BSL-2 also marks the start of restricted laboratory access to prevent outsiders from accidentally contracting these disease organisms.

Biosafety Level Three laboratories are designed to contain microbes that cause serious illness or death and can be transmitted through the air. *Mycobacterium tuberculosis*, the bacterium that causes tuberculosis, is one of these, as is the virus that causes a deadly brain infection called St. Louis encephalitis. To prevent these microbes from getting out of control, BSL-3 facilities have special ventilation systems that reduce the air pressure in the laboratory to keep unfiltered air from escaping from the lab. Of course, the air in the lab eventually has to return to the outer world, but air filters remove any pathogens before they can leave the building.

Biosafety Level Four laboratories contain the most deadly microbes, such as the viruses that cause Ebola and smallpox. These are diseases that are likely to lead to rapid death and for which a cure probably does not exist. To contain these organisms, BSL-4 labs are as isolated from the outside world as technology permits. Elaborate procedures protect the researchers that work in these labs. In a BSL-4 lab, microbes may be placed in separate isolation boxes or chambers with remote-operated robotic arms or permanently mounted gloves to enable the researchers to manipulate them while minimizing the risk of contamination.

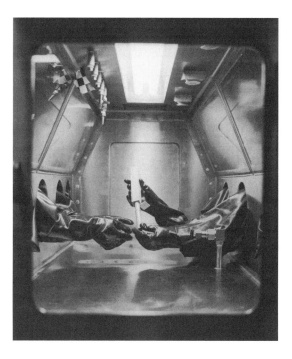

This unit was part of the CDC's Biosafety Level 4 (BSL-4), or maximum containment facility, in 1978. [Courtesy of Betty Partin, Centers for Disease Control and Prevention]

Tracking Diseases

Research into the causes of disease cannot take place solely within the safety of a laboratory. Diseases come from and affect life in the larger world—in big cities and in rural areas. Disease microbes may be found in ponds, under rocks, inside insects, in air-conditioning units, or underneath rugs. Nor are they alone; pathogens are generally surrounded by billions of harmless microbes. Locating and identifying disease microbes under these circumstances require special skills. The work is not without risk, but it is important: Disease microbes must be collected before they can be studied in the lab. And in order to understand these microbes, scientists must understand how they function in the larger environment.

Consider what happens when an unfamiliar disease makes its first appearance. The first challenge is simply to identify the presence of the microbe in the general population. In their early stages of infection, many microbes cause similar symptoms. Muscle aches and fever, for example, are as characteristic of the early stages of the flu as they are of smallpox. Unusual diseases are often initially misdiagnosed as a more common disease unless the patient is also exhibiting unusual symptoms. The physician's diagnosis is informed by what years of experience have taught him or her to expect to see. Commonly occurring symptoms generally elicit a common diagnosis. This is just as it should be. Physicians must, by necessity, work with only partial information. The fact remains, however, that misdiagnosing an unusual and infectious disease only delays a public-health response to the threat posed by the actual microbe.

Alternatively, a physician may encounter a single patient with unusual symptoms. Other physicians, perhaps located hundreds of miles apart, may each have a single patient displaying the same unusual symptoms. A single anomalous case is not usually enough to warrant investigation, but a collection of isolated cases may elicit a public-health response. The challenge, then, is to recognize the pattern in the data that will lead to identification of an epidemic in its early stages. The faster an outbreak of a disease can be identified, the better the chances of containing it within a small population.

Most developed countries have a national agency that attempts to identify and contain disease outbreaks. In the United States, the Centers for Disease Control and Prevention (CDC) in Atlanta, Georgia, an agency within the U.S. Department of Health, handles this task through its Epidemic Investigation Service (EIS). The EIS is a team of infectious-disease specialists who travel throughout the United States and to foreign countries to study and fight diseases. These scientists work with local physicians and governments, providing specialized experience and research capability that might be otherwise unavailable.

When working outside the lab at a location where the disease-causing microbe is endemic, researchers are at risk. To minimize this risk, researchers must find ways to isolate themselves from the microbe. They may build a biohazard research lab on-site, and they may choose to use various types of protective gear when out in the field.

Setting up a secure field laboratory is hard work. If a disease is serious enough to require BSL-4 containment, for example, researchers have to line each workroom with a system of plastic enclosures and tunnels to isolate the microbes. Each chamber must be equipped with its own portable ventilation system as well as airlocks to prevent the disease organisms from escaping. With the right equipment, such facilities can be nearly as secure as a full BSL-4 lab. They can even serve as hospital rooms for patients who need to be isolated from the outside world.

When in the field collecting microbes, researchers must do what they can to isolate themselves. Depending on how dangerous the disease seems to be, the researchers wear protective clothing ranging from respirators and rubber gloves to more rugged versions of a BSL-4 "moon suit." This gear allows the scientists to examine patients, collect water samples and other material, and perform other tasks without coming into direct contact with the pathogen.

Researchers and physicians undertake all of this effort in order to accomplish three basic goals: (1) identify the microbe causing the disease, (2) assist those already infected, and (3) contain the outbreak. Containment is especially important because the threats posed by many diseases will disappear once the microbes that cause them cannot be transmitted to new hosts. Containing an outbreak—preventing transmission of a microbe to new hosts—involves a good deal of detective work. Researchers seek to identify who first became ill with the disease and how that person contracted the microbes responsible. From that point, the researchers have to identify the pattern of transmission and track down everybody who might have been exposed to

A CDC scientist conducts laboratory research in the CDC's modern Biosafety Level 4 laboratory. [Courtesy of Centers for Disease Control and Prevention]

A public-health adviser conducting an interview in a disease-stricken community. Such advisers are called upon during public-health emergencies because of their ability and willingness to go into difficult and potentially dangerous situations to work with affected individuals. [Courtesy of Centers for Disease Control and Prevention]

the microbes, whether or not they show symptoms. The strategy behind the detective work is to identify all potential human vectors and place them under observation (or, in extreme cases, place them under quarantine) until the danger of further infections is passed.

Quarantine and Treatment

As the monkeypox outbreak of 2002 showed, quarantine is sometimes the best way to gain control over an epidemic. Keeping infected people isolated from the general population until they cease to be infectious may seem harsh, but it can be a very effective way to prevent the disease-causing microbe from finding new hosts in which to grow. Drugs are effective only when the microbe is vulnerable to an existing medication. Until physicians and health authorities know which, if any, drugs can combat a disease organism, the best thing they can do is stop the disease from spreading.

Quarantines are common in the modern world. Every year, millions of people informally quarantine themselves by staying home from school or work when they become ill. Hospitals set aside isolation rooms for patients who contract particularly infectious diseases. Even imported animals and plants are put into quarantine by national customs agencies until they can be tested for harmful microbes or observed for signs of infection. Quarantining patients during a disease outbreak is a much more serious matter. During the monkeypox outbreak, some patients' homes were kept under guard, both to keep any of the occupants from leaving and to prevent sympathetic family and friends from visiting. The only visitors allowed were the health workers who treated the patients and determined when it was safe to lift the quarantine.

Quarantines are not foolproof, and sometimes they are even counterproductive. For instance, measles is an illness caused by a virus. It is extremely contagious, and before a measles vaccine became widely available most children contracted it. The measles virus causes fevers, a runny nose, and a pink rash that covers the entire body. While the virus has always posed a serious health risk for some—it is occasionally fatal—most children who contract measles are sick for a few weeks and then recover with no complications. Furthermore, one does not get sick twice with measles. A single infection confers lifelong immunity. Finally, because measles was once so widespread (it is still common in areas of the world without mass vaccination programs), the chances of contracting it were virtually 100 percent.

In the days before measles vaccinations, there were two contrasting views of measles. Parents recognized that the disease probably posed no serious health risk for their child and, in any case, was almost inevitable. The only aspect of the disease that could be controlled was the timing of the infection. Some health departments recognized the disease as a threat to the public health. Consequently, they quarantined, or at least posted warning notices on, the homes of measles patients. Both perceptions were correct, but taken together they led to a peculiar and contradictory response to the disease.

Rather than preventing the spread of measles, warning notices and quarantine signs sometimes served as advertisements. Once a measles warning sign went up on a house, other parents in the neighborhood would bring their otherwise healthy children by to visit their sick friend, contract the disease, and acquire the immunity. Better to acquire it when they are young and healthy than later, when the situation may be less certain, was how the thinking went.

Because of past experiences with quarantines, governments today are more circumspect about the use of this technique to control the movements of microorganisms by controlling the movements of their hosts. They now generally reserve quarantine only for the most serious of diseases. Nevertheless, quarantines continue to be a valuable technique in the struggle to control the spread of disease.

BIOHAZARDS IN THE MODERN WORLD

With the discovery in 1928 of the antibiotic *penicillin* by Sir Alexander Fleming, people's perception of disease began to change. Many serious diseases were, with penicillin, not just curable but *easily* curable. Some health experts confidently predicted a future free of disease.

Nor was optimism about the future driven solely by advances within the field of medicine. Large-scale civil-engineering projects had a profound impact on the public health. As early as the 1880s, large cities built and improved water systems that dramatically reduced the amount of naturally occurring microbes in the water supply. New sewer systems ensured that wastes did not mix with drinking water or get discharged into the streets, as often happened in past centuries. And improved public sanitation services, from garbage collection to regularly scheduled street cleaning, removed many of the incubation sites of illness and the vermin that spread them.

All of these factors led to a decrease in disease and a corresponding increase in life expectancy. The populations of the United States, Europe, and a few other developed regions increased as a result. Other regions of the world experienced similar changes as these services and technologies made their way across the globe. Before long, dozens of diseases that had periodically devastated cities were no longer a threat. It is understandable that people thought that a final victory over disease was just a few decades away. Time has proved otherwise.

Anthrax in an Envelope

An epidemic can move fast enough to overwhelm public-health systems when microbes simply hop from one infected individual to the next available victim. When human beings decide to spread diseases deliberately, the effects can be devastating.

Bioterrorism—using disease microbes to cause widespread sickness, death, and fear—can be far more effective than terrorist attacks involving car bombs. The anthrax letter attack of 2001 demonstrated the dangers of bioterrorism. A week after the terrorist attacks of September 11, a trio of letters showed up at the Washington, D.C., offices of U.S. Senator Tom Daschle, the leader of the Senate's Democratic minority, at the New York offices of NBC News, addressed to anchorman Tom Brokaw, and at the offices of the *New York Post*. Each of these letters bore a false return address. The letter to Senator Daschle said, in part, "You cannot stop us. We have this anthrax. You die now." Each letter contained spores, or dormant forms, of a bacterium called *Bacillus anthracis*, the microbe that causes

One of the anthrax-containing envelopes used during the 2001 anthrax attack
[Topham/The Image Works]

anthrax. (Under certain conditions, anthrax bacteria produce spores that can remain dormant for long periods of time but become highly infectious under the right conditions.)

Anthrax is a potentially fatal disease. It can strike the skin, the lungs, or the gastrointestinal tract, depending on where the bacteria come into contact with the body. The inhaled form of anthrax is the most serious. (The name "anthrax" comes from *anthrakis*, the Greek word for coal, because of the black sores people get on their skin from the contact form of the disease.)

The letters contained anthrax spores that had been *weaponized*, processed into a form that could more easily be dispersed into the air and so more easily inhaled. Military researchers in several countries have developed these and other weapons-grade microbes for use in *biological* or *germ warfare*, both to sicken enemy troops and to devastate enemy nations. In their weaponized form, the anthrax bacteria constitute an extremely fine powder similar to flour or talcum powder.

Whoever sent the letters (the terrorist had not been caught as of the end of 2005) had included a small amount of the powderlike spores. The spores dispersed into the air when each envelope was opened. The goal of processing anthrax in this form is to cause the inhalation form of the disease. Inhalation anthrax is generally fatal when left untreated. The treatment is a course of antibiotics as soon as infection is suspected. The spores had begun to disperse, however, before the letters reached their destination. The envelopes had leaked as they went through the sorting machines of the United States Postal Service. Each of these high-speed machines process tens of thousands of letters each hour. The machines move the letters along via belts. The letters are bent around corners, past optical character readers, and ejected forcefully into trays that are ordered by zip code. This type of processing involves considerable bending and squeezing of the envelopes. It should have come as no surprise to find that some of the powder leaked out of the envelopes and spread into the machinery, onto other envelopes, and into the air of the sorting facilities.

By the time health authorities realized what was happening, several people in and outside the Postal Service were exhibiting symptoms of anthrax infection. Nineteen people developed one of the three forms of anthrax within a few of weeks after the letters were mailed; five died. But the effects of the attack went further: Because no one knew how many people might have been exposed to the powder, health authorities advised that office workers, postal workers, and anybody else who could be identified as possibly having come in contact with the powdered microbes should take a powerful antibiotic as a preventative measure. In the end, more than 30,000 people took antibiotics in case they, too, might be carrying the deadly germs. The anthrax letters showed how disruptive and deadly it could be to turn the machinery of the modern world into a delivery system for disease. (Chapter 9 discusses bioterrorism and biological weapons in greater detail.)

From the Western Nile to Middle America

When microbes and the hosts upon which they prey come into contact, disease can result. Sometimes the microbes are able to overcome the host's defenses, and the host becomes sick. Other times, the host's defenses may prove too strong and the microbe is repelled or destroyed. There is, however, a third, possibility: Sometimes the microbe is able to overcome the host's defenses and reproduce while causing few if any symptoms. In this case neither host nor microbe is injured.

The *West Nile virus* is sometimes an example of this process in action. Most people (approximately 80 percent) who come in contact with these microbes show no signs of infection. Symptoms, among those who exhibit them, are often no more severe than a mild case of the flu, and, indeed, the West Nile virus is sometimes misdiagnosed as the flu. (This group includes most of the remaining 20 percent of the infected population.) There are, however, some who are particularly susceptible to the effects of the virus. For these individuals, the West Nile virus can be fatal. (Individuals with serious symptoms comprise less than 1 percent of all those infected with the virus.) From 1999 to the end of 2003, 510 people in the United States died from the disease, according to the National Institutes of Health.

The year 1999 is the starting point for West Nile record keeping in the United States because that is the year the microbe was first identified in that nation—specifically, in New York City. West Nile is native to Africa; its name refers to scientists' first description of the virus during or just after an outbreak along the Nile River in eastern Africa. The virus also appears elsewhere throughout Africa, having traveled from host to host with the help of a mosquito called *Anopheles aegypti*. For years, the Atlantic Ocean served as an effective barrier to the disease's progress, but eventually an infected host—it is not known which species of host—reached New York.

Aedes albopictus mosquito, a vector for West Nile virus, feeding on human host [Courtesy of James Gathany, Centers for Disease Control and Prevention]

From that point, the virus spread steadily across the nation. As in Africa, mosquitoes transferred the disease from host to host with their bites. Birds such as crows helped carry the virus for miles, while horses also served as reservoirs for the microbes. Birds and horses are also vulnerable to the disease. By finding and examining dead birds and horses, researchers could track the path of the disease and provide some warning for people who lived in areas where the disease had arrived.

West Nile virus was able to entrench itself throughout the nation within five years, appearing in most of the continental United States by 2003. Its ability to infect birds ensured that it spread as quickly as the birds could fly. Its ability to exist in the bodies of several different species of animals, wild and domestic, has made it extremely difficult to control.

It is not known how the virus made its way into the United States. Perhaps an airplane or a ship brought an infected mosquito to the United States. New York City is an important port city, as well as being a major hub for international airplane flights, so it is not surprising that the West Nile virus first appeared there. The precise mechanism by which this virus crossed the Atlantic may, however, never be discovered.

Another example of this high-speed disease transfer took place in 2003. SARS, or severe acute respiratory syndrome, is a pneumonia-like illness that first appeared in rural China before spreading to urban centers such as Beijing and Hong Kong in February. Although its symptoms are similar to pneumonia, SARS is far deadlier, killing nearly 10 percent of those it infects. By the time SARS was correctly identified—as a virus new to humans—travelers had taken it to some of the major cities of Canada, the United States, and other nations.

Canada in particular saw the most dramatic anti-SARS measure: the quarantine of Toronto in March and April by the *World Health Organization*. The health agency quarantined Toronto because it had the highest number of SARS cases outside China. For two months, no airplanes could land in the city unless they were carrying passengers who absolutely needed to be there. By the end of the quarantine, Toronto had lost billions of dollars in tourism and other business.

Both the West Nile virus and the international SARS outbreak show, not only how easily microbes can be transported to new regions of the world, but also how rapidly these globe-hopping epidemics can disrupt life and business. In these two cases, however, the outbreaks have had a limited effect. Other newcomer microbes, however, had long-lasting effects not just on individual nations but also on the world.

HIV/AIDS

Acquired immunodeficiency syndrome, known by its acronym AIDS, is one of the most notorious diseases of the 20th century. The human immunodeficiency virus (HIV), the virus that causes AIDS, has proven particularly resistant to attempts to control it or to cure the disease that it causes. HIV can take a decade or longer to have a visible effect, and its victims can live for years before succumbing. As a result, an infected individual can spread the virus to many people before showing any sign of infection. By the end of 2003, an estimated 40 million people around the world, including 1 million in the United States, either carried HIV or had AIDS.

Though most people think of AIDS as a sexually transmitted disease or one that is transmitted when drug addicts share needles, it seems to have begun as a threat to African hunters searching for food. HIV is very similar to a microbe called simian immunodeficiency virus, or SIV, that infects some species of monkeys in central Africa. AIDS researchers who have studied the two viruses and who have traced the history of AIDS think that the human version of the disease may have developed from the simian form. It is likely that a mutant form of SIV found its way into a hunter's or a cook's body through a scratch or a cut while a day's catch was being prepared. The virus was able to reproduce in its new host's body, adapting to its new environment and exploiting human behavior to spread itself to a greater number of people.

AIDS first came to the world's attention in the early 1980s, but researchers think it appeared far earlier—possibly as early as the mid-

1950s. They came to this conclusion after searching through health records collected by international health organizations that worked in Africa, such as the United Nations' World Health Organization (WHO). The researchers found files that described symptoms similar to those of AIDS in people living in areas where SIV was endemic. Physicians of that time did not know that SIV existed. They misdiagnosed their patients' maladies as an unusual strain of an identified local disease or failed to decide on a diagnosis. Because a pattern was not recognized, no further investigation was made into these cases at the time.

Over the years, HIV evolved and spread throughout much of the continent. It moved from host to host without causing much concern, thanks, in part, to its years-long incubation period. Once again, modern transportation systems helped spread the disease. By the time people recognized HIV/AIDS as the health threat that it is, it was already a global pandemic.

Three factors prevented medical researchers from identifying AIDS more rapidly than they did. First, as previously mentioned, the

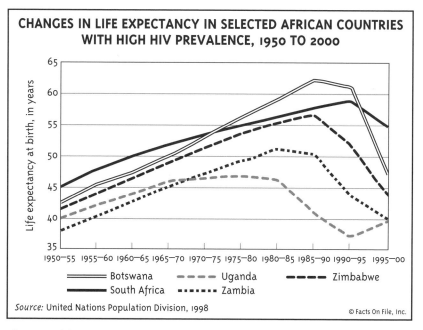

CHANGES IN LIFE EXPECTANCY IN SELECTED AFRICAN COUNTRIES WITH HIGH HIV PREVALENCE, 1950 TO 2000

Life expectancy at birth, in years

Botswana ─── Uganda ─ ─ ─ Zimbabwe ▬ ▬ ▬
South Africa ▬▬▬ Zambia ▪▪▪▪▪▪▪

Source: United Nations Population Division, 1998

© Facts On File, Inc.

Changes in life expectancy in African countries with high HIV infection rates. Because HIV often affects otherwise healthy young adults, its effect on life expectancy is especially dramatic.

disease has a long incubation time. Second, the effect of the virus itself is complex. People with AIDS often die of other conditions. The HIV virus interferes with a type of immune cell called a T cell, which it uses in its own reproductive cycle. The function of T cells is to identify microbial invaders within the body, triggering the immune system into action. If HIV disrupts enough T cells, the immune system does not recognize these other, foreign microbes, which then take advantage of the opportunity to grow within the infected individual's body. These opportunistic diseases—such as pneumonia and Kaposi's sarcoma, a form of skin cancer—are often what kill AIDS patients. Finally, there has historically been less interest on the part of researchers and pharmaceutical companies in diseases that are restricted to developing nations, and HIV/AIDS arose in a region that is generally poor and without a well-developed public-health system. Nearly 28 million people around the world, including nearly 500,000 in the United States, have died from AIDS in the two decades since the disease was first identified. As an overall cause of death, AIDS ranks far below such maladies as cancer or heart disease.

AIDS is only the most recent pandemic to afflict millions of people around the world. It is by no means the first nor is there any reason to suspect that it will be the last. The challenge, then, is to better understand the nature of diseases and the mechanisms by which they can be transmitted so that the damage done by these microbes can be minimized.

PART 2

Biohazards throughout History

5

THE GREAT PLAGUES

In previous centuries, disease and death were often more familiar parts of life than they are today. Child mortality rates were much higher. Life expectancies were lower. At different times and in different places, outbreaks of plague, smallpox, *cholera, yellow fever,* and other diseases would sweep through the population, causing widespread suffering and death. Other contagious diseases, such as tuberculosis, were ever-present—so familiar, in fact, that writers used them as plot devices in their books, plays, and operas. *La Bohème,* an opera by Giacomo Puccini from the 1890s, featured a character whose death by tuberculosis was the story's central tragedy.

The great plagues of history caused more than isolated individual tragedies. They sometimes changed the course of history. They affected the development of nations. The following short list covers a few of the human race's most deadly encounters with contagious diseases and conveys some idea of how difficult it was, sometimes, to simply survive.

The Black Death

When viewed through a microscope there is nothing especially noteworthy about the *Yersinia pestis* bacterium. It is a simple-looking

αιbiti anno ρediüo g̃ ĩ die ceρeruut coɱρᷓti ρerſoiiis ē
aɫɫumptionis iiirguiis gloꝛ ꝑuiriienne counoolere eti deo gꝛa
oſe veneviint a uilla bꝛuigen tias redtere ſuꝑeꝛ tanta ꝑenı
ſi aꝛater.cc. hominꝛꝰ: quaſi ×oꝛa renaa quam grauiſſimam re

This picture from 1349 shows the Brothers of the Cross scourging themselves as they walk through the Dutch town of Doornik in an attempt to free the world from the plague. [AAPL/Topham/The Image Works]

pin-shaped germ. But the seemingly unremarkable *Y. pestis* has long been a plague on the human race. In fact, the bacterium *Y. pestis* is the original plague on humanity. (The word "plague" once referred just to the diseases that this bacteria causes; later, it came to mean any widespread disease or catastrophe.) Few epidemics have killed more people at one time or caused as much social disruption as *Y. pestis*.

The single symptom most often associated with the plague is a swollen, tender lymph gland, also called a lymph node. (The lymph glands are part of the immune system.) When the lymph gland becomes swollen, it is called a bubo. Other symptoms include fever, extreme fatigue, and chills. Symptoms generally appear within a week after the individual is infected. This is called bubonic plague, after the telltale bubo.

As the plague bacteria continue to reproduce, they overwhelm the immune system and begin to multiply in the blood. Once in the circulatory system, they spread rapidly throughout the body. When the bacteria infect the lungs, breathing becomes difficult. (This is called pneumonic plague.) After the lungs are infected, the condition of the individual deteriorates rapidly. The disease is usually fatal. (Modern antibiotics are effective against *Y. pestis.*)

The plague inspired fear in a way that few diseases have. The appearance of the bubos is rapid and dramatic. The mortality rates were very high, and absent a correct theory of disease, there was no explanation for the plague's sudden appearance. But even to those living in the Middle Ages, there were hints about the nature of the disease.

The plague is not a disease specific to humans. Rodents serve as a nonhuman reservoir for the bacterium, but they, too, are susceptible to the effects of the germ. And because medieval standards of hygiene were not especially high—various forms of waste were often removed from the home by simply tossing them out the window—rats were commonplace. There are historical accounts of large numbers of rats dying just before the plague appeared among humans. There were those who suspected that the Black Death, as it came to be called, was associated with rats, and large numbers of dead and dying rats meant that the plague was among them even when no humans showed signs of the disease yet.

Often the strategy employed by Europeans to fight the plague was to quarantine those who were sick. A strategy of quarantine indicates that some medieval Europeans ascribed the plague to some agent that could be physically contained: They must have attributed the plague to a physical agent, or they would not have attempted to contain it physically. Of course, there were other explanations at the time, including appeals to supernatural forces, but the fact that some tried to contain the disease through a policy of quarantine is proof that at least some were thinking in terms of cause and effect.

The quarantines were not very effective. Precisely the same bacterium that infected the humans infected the rodents, and so human-to-human contact was not necessary to transmit the disease. All that was needed was a vector to transfer the germ from the **rats to** the humans; the vector was a flea. The fleas were parasitic; they fed on the blood of both humans and rats. They could leave one host after feeding and later attach themselves to a different host to feed again. The microbe was transferred in the process of feeding. Given the hygiene standards of the time, it is doubtful that many people would have been either surprised or dismayed to discover fleas in their clothing or their bedding. Neither would they have been surprised to find rats in their dwellings. Consequently, the bacteria, if not the human hosts, were able to evade the quarantine.

It should be noted, however, that there was, nevertheless, some value to quarantine. Pneumonic plague occurs when *Y. pestis* infects the lungs. One of the symptoms is coughing, and when the infected person coughs, the bacterium is expelled into the air. If it is inhaled, it can infect another person. Quarantine limits the opportunities for this type of transmission to occur.

The plague's combination of stealth and speed made it one of the most deadly diseases in history. The most well-known outbreak took place in Europe during the 14th century from 1347 to 1351. Called the Black Death, the plague killed 25 million people, wiping out many communities and reducing Europe's population by perhaps 50 percent. (The lack of records makes an exact figure impossible to obtain.)

It is interesting to note that the plague may have been introduced into Europe as a bioweapon. Some historians trace the introduction of the plague into European populations when plague-infested corpses were catapulted into a Genoese trading outpost located in the Crimea, located by the Black Sea in southern Ukraine. Genoa is today a city and province in Italy. The attack on the Genoese outpost was carried out by the Kipchaks, members of a loosely organized confederation that occupied a large area of the Asian steppe. Some of the Genoese later sailed back to Genoa, and as they made the long journey home, they stopped in ports along the way and left behind the plague. Most of the ship's occupants had died of the plague by the time the ship reached their homeport. Recognizing the danger, the ship was ordered to sea, but it was too late. They had brought the plague home, and this biological attack on a distant outpost of a single European nation may have resulted in one of the worst pandemics in history.

By the end of the 14th century's plague outbreak, so many people had died throughout Europe that the course of history itself changed. Wars between the many small nations of Europe ceased, if only briefly. The level of trade between nations also diminished. The survivors found themselves living in a new kind of society: For centuries the lives of Europeans had been largely determined by the social class into which they were born, and although the Black Death did not eliminate the class system, it did change it. Many of the surviving landowners saw their fortunes vanish because there were not enough laborers left to tend the fields. Many of the surviving villagers, recognizing that there were too few people left alive to sustain their village, moved to the larger cities. In England alone, for example, it is estimated that approximately 1,000 villages ceased to exist because of the plague. So many people died that more than a century would pass before the population of Europe again reached its pre-plague level.

Smallpox in the New World

The Black Plague was particularly well documented, but it was not unique in the extent of its destruction. In most other respects, what happened with the plague has been repeated elsewhere. Even in terms of the terrible toll it took on a large population (Europeans) dispersed over an entire continent (Europe), there is at least one other similar case.

"New" populations—that is, populations that have had no previous exposure to a pathogen—are often, as previously mentioned, the most susceptible to its effects. When no individual in an entire population has developed immunity to a particular pathogen, all adults and all children are susceptible, and when virtually everyone is sick, there is no one left to tend the crops, defend the nation's borders, or aid the sick. The disease that creates these conditions rends the social fabric of the nation it infects. Often the introduction of microbes virulent enough to alter the course of history has happened unintentionally. But it has happened often enough for many historians and anthropologists to call disease organisms the conqueror's hidden ally and the conquered's hidden foe.

Perhaps the most extreme interaction between disease and human history took place after the European discovery of the Caribbean Sea and the Americas. Hungry for land, wealth, and power, the seagoing kingdoms of Spain and Portugal divided this new world between them, setting up colonies to gather its riches and send them across the Atlantic Ocean. Spain's holdings were by far the larger of the two. The Aztecs, the Incas, and the other peoples who were already using this "New World wealth" for themselves naturally tried to stop the Spanish conquistadors from putting this plan into effect. Even as they prepared to defend themselves, however, their societies were nearly destroyed by the diseases that the Europeans unwittingly introduced.

The worst of the imported diseases was smallpox, which had never been seen before in the Western Hemisphere. Poxes of all kinds—which got their name from the pockets of pus that formed on the skin—were common throughout Europe. Smallpox, a disease that killed millions of Europeans every century, was the deadliest form, but there also were less-harmful versions such as chickenpox and cowpox.

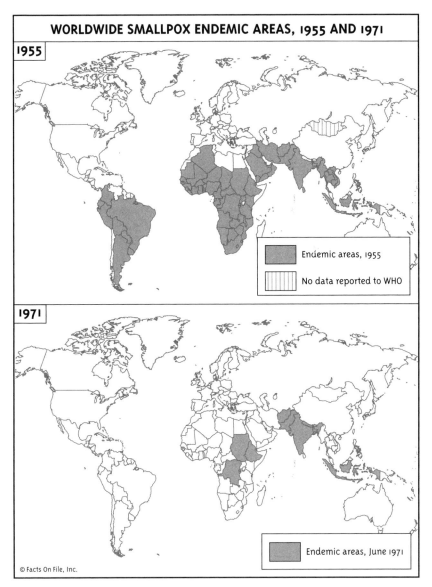

Smallpox was brought rapidly under control by the World Health Organization.
Notice the tremendous reduction in range between 1955 and 1971. The last naturally
occurring case of smallpox was in 1977.

Unfortunately, it was the smallpox virus that reached the New World,
and from the 1520s onward it spread rapidly throughout North, Central, and South America, aided by additional transmissions from Eng-

lish, Dutch, and French colonists as their nations successfully broke the Spanish/Portuguese lock on travel to North America and the Caribbean.

Without the presence of smallpox, the Indian inhabitants of the New World would have had a difficult time resisting the technological superiority of the invaders. Smallpox, however, often made effective resistance impossible. Too many died, and the rest were often too weak to resist. Researchers now estimate the death toll among indigenous peoples of North and South America at about 50 percent. Some estimate that it was substantially higher. The disease quickly spread to areas where European explorers had yet to travel, particularly in parts of what became the southern United States. There are affecting accounts of explorers entering a village for the first time and finding it already abandoned, its population decimated by the new diseases.

Smallpox's devastation of the New World continued for centuries. As late as 1837, a smallpox outbreak struck the Arikara, Hidatsa, and Mandan tribes along the Missouri River, killing roughly 15,000 people. Settlers and their descendants were not invulnerable either. During 1689, more than 1,000 of the nearly 57,000 residents of the Massachusetts Colony died from the disease. Large cities such as New York, Boston, and Chicago were scenes of occasional, more circumscribed epidemics until the 20th century. As late as 1967, smallpox caused an estimated 2 million deaths worldwide. Efforts by the United Nations' World Health Organization resulted in the eradication of the disease. It now survives at two research laboratories on opposite sides of the globe. (See chapter 9.)

Cholera, Tuberculosis, and Other Foes

Smallpox and the plague have special places in history because they killed so many people in such a short span that they altered the course of history. But the catalog of biohazardous organisms includes many other devastating microbes. Some of these other organisms caused pandemics that were somewhat similar to the epidemics of plague and smallpox described earlier—at least in the sense of alarm they caused, if not in the mortality that resulted. Others were (and in some areas of the world remain) continual sources of mortality in the same way that heart disease and cancer are currently continuous sources of mortality in developed nations. In earlier centuries, however, there was no real understanding of the nature of the disease or the mechanisms by which they were transmitted. The result was that by today's standards, at least, the people of earlier times were often remarkably fatalistic about disease and its consequences.

It is important to emphasize that some of these diseases are with us still. Tuberculosis and malaria, in particular, still devastate some parts of the world. That these two diseases no longer receive the attention that they once did reflects the fact that they have been largely eradicated from developed nations. But out of sight of the world's television cameras, millions of people continue to suffer and die from these maladies. Finally, because most of the people who die from these diseases are poor, pharmaceutical companies have historically shown little interest in developing new classes of drugs that might help. There is simply not enough profit to make the development of such drugs financially attractive—better to develop drugs for hair loss and sexual impotence; these are proven moneymakers. Nevertheless, understanding how historically important diseases affected people in the past illustrates why it is important to continue efforts to better control—and, where possible, eradicate—them.

Cholera is an infection of the upper intestines by the bacterium *Vibrio cholerae*, which lurks in water or food that is contaminated by fecal matter, or in some types of raw or undercooked seafood. Symptoms of cholera include severe diarrhea and vomiting, which leads to rapid dehydration and sometimes death. The onset of the symptoms is sudden and dramatic and cholera outbreaks sometimes caused widespread panic.

Today we know that cholera is caused by the bacterium *Vibrio cholerae*, which creates an infection in the small intestine. The cholera germ is usually ingested by eating contaminated food or, more commonly, drinking contaminated water. The bacterium releases a toxin, and it is this toxin that causes violent diarrhea and vomiting. The shock to the body of losing three to four gallons (15–20 L) or more of fluids in a 24-hour period is often fatal.

For most of human history, cholera was endemic to the Indian subcontinent. It usually appears suddenly, often in crowded conditions, and spreads rapidly throughout the population, causing thousands of deaths before quickly fading away. In a well-documented 1781 outbreak in the Indian city of Hardiwar, 20,000 people died in eight days. Early in the 19th century, however, the geographical pattern of transmission changed as cholera spread around the planet during a series of pandemics. Europe, China, Australia, North and South America, and Africa all saw cholera epidemics for the first time. Millions died.

Virtually all large-scale outbreaks are testimony to poor sanitation. Because the cholera germ is contracted by ingesting it—usually through a contaminated water supply—the surest strategy for preventing cholera epidemics is to prevent its transmission by providing clean drinking water. (Today cholera is also easily treatable.) In developed nations, cholera is now almost entirely a disease of the past. Its continued presence in developing nations illustrates the extremely difficult conditions under which many people still live. In fact, some of the worst outbreaks in modern times have occurred in refugee camps among those fleeing war. Because cholera is easily preventable and easily curable, there is no technical reason why it cannot be removed as a large-scale health threat. It is worth noting, however, that *Vibrio cholerae* can live in nonhuman hosts, including some shellfish. As a consequence, it can only be controlled, not eradicated.

Tuberculosis has always been a major source of mortality. It is primarily a lung infection caused by the *Mycobacterium tuberculosis* bacteria. The most common way to contract tuberculosis is to inhale bacteria that have been coughed or sneezed out by someone who suffers from the disease. Crowded conditions make it easy for tuberculosis to jump from person to person.

In the past, tuberculosis was a major killer in virtually every nation. Millions of people died from tuberculosis each year, and it affected people from all walks of life. The American novelist Robert Louis Stevenson (1850–94) had tuberculosis, as did the Polish composer Frédéric Chopin (1810–49) and the Norwegian mathematician Niels Hendrik Abel (1802–29). Those with sufficient money went to specialized hospitals called sanitariums that catered to people who had the disease. The sanitariums were usually located where (according to theory of the time) patients would benefit from exposure to the fresh air of the countryside. From the late 18th to the early 20th century, tuberculosis—also called TB or consumption because it seemed to slowly devour its victims—was a major health risk everywhere.

In the West during the 19th century, tuberculosis was the single-leading cause of death among all age groups, accounting for one death out of every seven. The introduction of antibiotics and an increase in the standard of living during the first half of the 20th century drastically cut down the number of tuberculosis cases in developed nations. Globally, however, TB remains the second-leading cause of death by infectious disease. Today 2 million people die of TB or related complications each year.

Malaria is another devastating disease that is now largely confined to the developing world. This disease is the result of an infection by a parasite called plasmodium, a wormlike microorganism that affects the body's red blood cells. The malaria vector, or method of transmission, is the infected female *Anopheles* mosquito, which transmits the malaria parasite as it removes blood from its human victim. The disease's symptoms are marked by high fever, severe chills, anemia (an inability of the blood to carry oxygen), jaundice, enlargement of the spleen, and complications arising from the initial symptoms.

Throughout history, malaria has been one of the most lethal of diseases. There are several strains of the disease, some of which are more severe in their effects than others. Generally speaking, falciparum, the most lethal strain of the disease, is confined to the tropics. At one time, malaria was a significant source of mortality in a broad region that included parts of the southern United States. Unlike smallpox, malaria exists in nonhuman hosts as well as human ones. Rats, birds, and monkeys are some of the other organisms capable of harboring the malarial parasite. As a consequence, the parasite probably cannot be eliminated from the environment in the near future. Because no vaccine currently exists, it will likely continue to pose a health threat for some time.

Developed nations have, however, been very successful in controlling malaria. While drugs exist that can alleviate symptoms and even prevent infection, the most effective public health measure has generally been to control the species of insect, the *Anopheles* mosquito, that spreads the disease. Historically, this has involved draining wetlands, and during the middle years of the 20th century, the newly developed pesticide DDT was applied liberally and regularly. As a result of these efforts, malaria was brought under control in those nations that could afford to do so. As with TB, there has been relatively little attention to malaria in the world media in recent years, and pharmaceutical companies have spent comparatively little money searching for ways to combat the disease. Also as with TB, today malaria is largely confined to the developing world, where it remains a significant source of mortality. An estimated 500 million people have the disease, and an estimated 1 million people die from it every year. In 2002, it was the fourth-leading cause of death among children in developing countries.

The last major killer on this brief list is yellow fever, which, like malaria, is transmitted from victim to victim through mosquito bites. In this case, the vector can be one of several species of mosquito. The symptoms of yellow fever occur abruptly and include fever, nausea, and

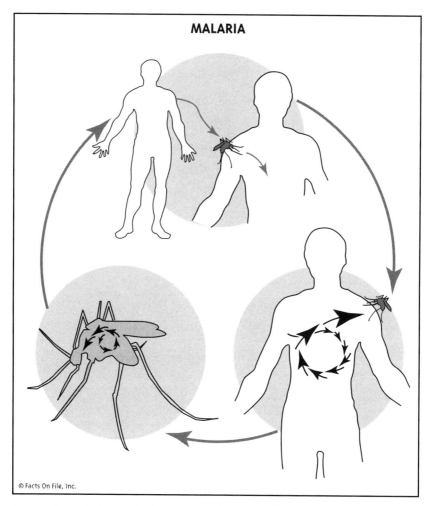

MALARIA

© Facts On File, Inc.

Because the malaria parasite infects mosquitoes as well as humans, it is easily transmissible. Malaria remains a major cause of sickness and death in large regions of the world.

vomiting. The virus destroys liver cells—one consequence of which is jaundice, which can be identified by the yellowing of the skin and eyes as bile accumulates in the body. (The symptoms of jaundice are what gave rise to the name of the disease.) One characteristic that yellow fever shares with smallpox is that if one survives the disease, one acquires immunity from further infection. This immune response has been used by scientists to create vaccines that enable the recipient to acquire the immune response without the illness. This technology, along with very aggressive programs of mosquito control, has greatly reduced the risk of the disease, but for centuries it was a major killer in large areas of the world. It is endemic to the tropics, but serious yellow fever epidemics have been recorded as far north as Boston, Massachusetts, before the disease was brought under control.

Yellow fever is also interesting for the methods used to investigate it. Because it was so deadly and widespread, there was great interest in identifying the mechanism by which it was transmitted. U.S. Army bacteriologist Walter Reed (1851–1902) and an army physician named John Carroll were assigned to investigate yellow fever. They eventually proved (by a series of experiments on human volunteers, including Carroll himself) that mosquitoes transmit the disease. Having identified the vector, the U.S. government undertook very aggressive programs of mosquito control in, for example, Panama, where yellow fever had impeded construction of the Panama Canal by sickening or killing the workers. These programs were successful and saved many lives. Although the yellow fever microbe can still be found in the wild, it has largely been eliminated as a threat to the public health.

EPIDEMICS AND PANDEMICS OF THE 20TH CENTURY

Infectious diseases have not stopped shaping world history simply because the human race has developed the medical knowledge it needs to identify and combat them. Microbes have been living in and feeding off higher organisms for millions of years. To live that long, they have had to adapt to constantly changing conditions in the microbe-hostile environment each body strives to maintain. As germs interact with their environment and create the next generation of microorganisms, the new microorganisms are sometimes a little different than their predecessors. Some of the new variants pose new threats to their human hosts. It is a relentless process, and it never stops.

The Influenza Pandemic of 1918

The influenza pandemic of 1918 and 1919 spread across the entire planet. It started several months before November 11, 1918, the official end of World War I. By the time the outbreak ended—and it is not at all clear why it ended—many more people had died of this strain of flu than had died from combat during four years of world war. The disease spread from China to Europe via commercial shipping. Late in the summer, soldiers in the trenches of France and southern Europe began to contract an especially virulent form of flu. Within months, the new strain of flu was firmly settled on both sides of the Atlantic Ocean, as servicemen and commercial sailors alike began carrying the virus to new hosts. Many people who had never been sick in their lives died from this strain of flu.

Influenza pandemics were not new: In 1889 and 1890, a pandemic affected more than 40 percent of the world's population. The 1918 flu is historic because it was so deadly. There was great confusion about the origins of the disease. At the time, it was called the Spanish flu because the disease infected 80 percent of Spain's population and killed members of the Spanish royal family. Some among the Western allies initially thought it might be a final attempt by the Central Powers to win the war using germ warfare, but they soon learned that Germany, Austro-Hungary, and the Ottomans were hit as badly as those in the West.

Over the next year and a half, the flu killed between 20 million and 40 million people around the world. No place was far enough from the world's population centers to escape the pandemic. Small villages in the

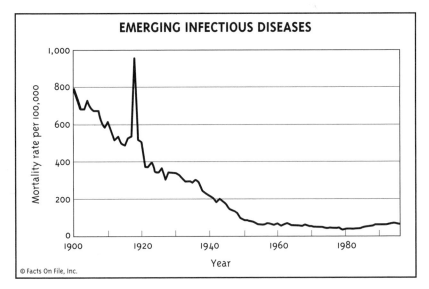

EMERGING INFECTIOUS DISEASES

© Facts On File, Inc.

Infectious disease has been a steadily decreasing cause of mortality in the United States throughout most of the 20th century. The large spike is due to the 1918 flu pandemic.

Advertisement during the influenza pandemic of 1918 [Topham/The Image Works]

north of Norway suffered losses to the flu, as did major cities such as New York, whose 19,000 flu deaths were just a small part of America's death toll of 500,000. Nearly 20 percent of the 38,000 inhabitants of Western Samoa in the South Pacific Ocean died, and the effect on the isolated villages of Alaska was also frequently devastating.

The flu ended as suddenly as it began, leaving the most important scientific questions unanswered: Where did this strain of flu originate? Why was this particular strain so much deadlier than other strains? Why did this deadly strain not reemerge the following year? Would a similarly deadly strain emerge in the future? And finally, what, if anything, could be done to protect the public health should this strain of flu reemerge?

There is still uncertainty about the nature of the so-called Spanish flu, but researchers have never given up hope of learning its secrets. Real progress in understanding the nature of flu as a general phenomenon occurred in the 1930s, when a British research team isolated the first sample of influenza virus. One year earlier, American researcher Richard Shope proved that influenza could be transferred from pigs to other animals. But progress in understanding the 1918 flu strain was hampered by lack of technology and lack of samples:

During the pandemic, few thought to save a sample of a flu patient's skin, blood, or other fluids for future study. Medical researchers eventually identified a region of China as the source of most flu strains, but no one was able to study the 1918 flu until the mid-1990s, when archaeologists exhumed the frozen remains of flu victims from some Norwegian villages north of the Arctic Circle. Finally, using recent breakthroughs in the science of genetics, researchers had the opportunity to see the 1918 virus itself. The 1918 flu pandemic continues to be an active area of research, as scientists strive to make scientific sense of what was arguably the most dangerous disease of the 20th century.

Polio

While the dangers of deadly, global pandemics are real, one should keep in mind that humanity is no longer helpless. Scientists have already learned to control some very dangerous diseases. Poliomyelitis, commonly known as *polio*, is a virus that attacks and inflames gray

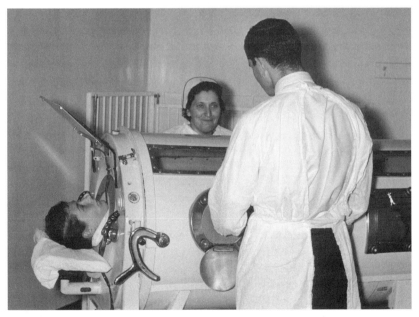

Hospital staff examining a polio patient who is encased in an early type of respirator called an iron lung [Courtesy of Centers for Disease Control and Prevention]

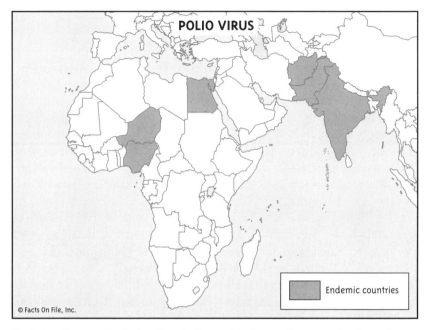

POLIO VIRUS

Endemic countries

© Facts On File, Inc.

Shaded regions are the last nations in the world where polio was endemic as of 2004. Elimination of the virus is anticipated in the next few years.

nerve tissue in the spinal cord. In its most serious manifestations, polio causes partial or total paralysis by destroying the brain's ability to communicate with the muscles. Polio has been brought under control.

It was during the 1950s that the major polio breakthroughs occurred. Prior to the 1950s, polio was widespread and deadly. During one nationwide outbreak in 1916, polio infected nearly 27,000 people, almost one-fifth of whom died. Perhaps the most well-known person to contract polio was Franklin Delano Roosevelt, the 32nd president of the United States, who came down with the disease in 1921 when he was 39 years old. The disease cost Roosevelt the use of his legs, forcing him to use a wheelchair for the rest of his life.

For decades, researchers searched for a polio vaccine, but they had no success until 1952, when U.S. researcher Dr. Jonas Salk developed a vaccine using viruses that he inactivated with a solution of formaldehyde. The outer shells of the inactivated viruses were intact, so that once injected, the body was able to develop an immune response to the active forms of the poliovirus. In 1954, after some preliminary tests (Salk and his family were some of the test subjects), elementary school students across the nation received the world's first polio vaccinations. The vaccine proved highly effective. There are three types of poliovirus, and Salk's vaccine effectively prepared the students' immune systems to destroy all three. It is worth noting that Salk gave away the vaccine. He never earned any money from it. When Salk was asked who owned this vaccine, he answered, "the people."

A few years later, a vaccine that used live poliovirus succeeded Salk's dead-virus vaccine. Dr. Albert Sabin, a Russian-born American physician and microbiologist, had been working with live polioviruses since the mid-1930s and was convinced that making a safe vaccine from live, but weakened, polioviruses was possible. And it would be cheaper and easier to give because it would not have to be injected; it could be ingested. By 1957, Sabin had created a vaccine from the three kinds of live polioviruses, and over the next two years gave it in sweet syrup or candy to children in Russia, Poland, Mexico, and Singapore. (He had to go outside the United States to test it because most American children had already been given Salk's vaccine.) Fifteen million children received Sabin's vaccine, with very few ill effects. In 1960, the U.S. government approved the oral vaccine, which was given out in sugar cubes rather than hypodermic needles. Since that time, polio has been eliminated in most areas of the world, thanks to an aggressive campaign of immunization coordinated by the World Health Organization (WHO). Polio continues to be a problem in certain areas of Africa where war makes it difficult to administer the vaccine or where there is suspicion of the motives of WHO.

Legionnaires' Disease

As familiar diseases are brought under control or eradicated, new ones come to the fore. In 1976, a deadly malady came to public attention for the first time when it appeared in the city of Philadelphia, Pennsylvania. The disease was similar to pneumonia. In addition to pneumonia, the symptoms included fever, abnormal liver function, and some mental confusion. It was deadly and unfamiliar. The initial outbreak consisted of 180 members of the American Legion, a nationwide organization of veterans, of whom 29 died. Many of the 29 deaths occurred because physicians, faced with a new infectious agent, were uncertain which antibiotic was effective. The mortality rate dropped after it was determined that the bacterium was susceptible to the antibiotic erythromycin.

To commemorate the bicentennial of the American Revolution, the American Legion was holding its annual convention in the city where the Declaration of Independence had been signed 200 years before. The group chose the Bellevue Stratford Hotel as its convention site, and many of the Legionnaires—as the members called themselves—stayed in the hotel during the four-day get-together. Aside from the Legionnaires, no one else came down with the disease. Consequently, the news media and health researchers began calling the malady "Legionnaire's disease."

Although the disease was new, the methods used to understand it were not. Researchers from the Centers for Disease Control and Prevention used standard *epidemiologic* concepts and methods to search for a cause. Medical examiners found unfamiliar bacteria in the lungs of the dead Legionnaires. Tests of the hotel kitchen failed to yield the same bacteria, and tests in other hotel rooms also failed to uncover the presence of the bacteria.

When Legionnaires' disease was first identified in the famous 1970s Philadelphia outbreak, there was widespread speculation about its cause. [Courtesy of Dr. Martin Hicklin, Centers for Disease Control and Prevention]

An especially observant infectious-disease specialist finally solved the mystery. The first day he arrived at the hotel, he noticed a trickle of water running down one side of the 72-year-old hotel. Like many older buildings, the hotel used a water-based air-conditioning system, rather than one that cooled the air using chemical refrigerants. The cooling system sent water in a closed loop over a network of pipes to remove heat from the air. The system's water reservoir, with its stable supply of warm water, made a perfect incubator for bacteria, including those now known as *Legionella pneumophila*, the microbe responsible for Legionnaire's disease.

The disease specialist realized that if water was leaking from the system to the outside of the hotel, it might also be leaking into the air ducts as well. From the ducts, the bacteria could loft into the air, and some of those bacteria might find their way into the lungs of members of the American Legion. An examination of the air-cooling system revealed that this method was exactly how the bacteria had reached the hotel's guests. The water in the cooling system was a rich soup of bacteria.

Having identified the cause of an unfamiliar disease, the next question of interest to researchers was whether *Legionella* was a new type of bacterium or whether past unexplained outbreaks of pneumonia-like disease could now be attributed to this pathogen. Research revealed that previously unexplained clusters of illness in Washington, D.C., Benidorm, Spain, and Nottingham, England, had all, in fact, been caused by *Legionella*. The bacterium had not been identified previously because researchers had not seen it. When searching for a microbe under a microscope, researchers use certain chemicals to stain the bacteria in order to make them easier to see. It is a peculiarity of the *Legionella* bacterium that it does not stain when the usual staining agents are applied.

7

EARLY ATTEMPTS
AT CONTAINMENT

One would think that before an epidemic can be contained researchers must understand the nature of the microbe responsible. Understanding what one is doing has never proved to be a hindrance, but experience has shown that deep insights into microbiology are neither necessary nor sufficient for the control of disease. (An extremely reliable method of controlling the transmission of smallpox—vaccination—was discovered long before the germ theory of disease was developed.)

Generally, however, researchers must know something about the mechanisms of transmission of the disease—possibly the ecology of the microbe; possibly, even, the physical structure of the microbe (for example, what the mechanism is that enables a microbe to evade the body's immune system). Knowledge of all these factors and others may prove to be important. But none of them, whether taken singly or in combination, is enough to ensure success. Historically, containing an epidemic has often depended on an uneven mix of science, common sense, and good fortune.

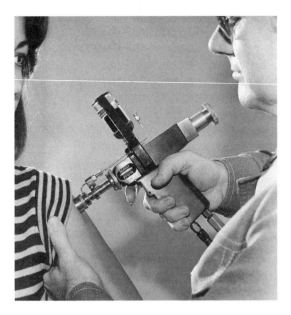

A "jet injector" is used to administer an influenza vaccine to prevent what many thought would be the next great flu pandemic, the so-called swine flu of 1976. (Courtesy of Robert E. Bates, Centers for Disease Control and Prevention)

Blockades against Infectious Disease

For most of humanity's existence, the only way to prevent epidemics from spreading was to physically block their path. A quarantine of individuals or small groups of sick people was one way to halt an outbreak. Some of the most drastic measures to isolate a population from disease took place during the days when cities protected themselves within gated walls. Faced with a deadly epidemic, the authorities—in the form of a kingdom's army—sometimes attempted to force the city's residents to remain behind the gates until the disease had run its course. For some, this proved to be a death sentence. The hope was that by containing the disease within the city walls, the larger population outside the gates would remain uninfected and safe.

In a similar vein, there have been times when townspeople in areas that had not yet been stricken with disease armed themselves and denied access to their towns to any refugees from areas already stricken. Gathering on the roads, they would force refugees from disease-ridden areas either to turn back or to head in a different direction. These measures helped some communities avoid major diseases but, again, at the expense of those seeking help.

More civilized times demanded more civilized ways of preventing the spread of disease. For centuries, monks and nuns in Europe cared for the sick in hospitals or small colonies that were far from cities and towns. Later, many public hospitals were established for similar reasons: Local governments set up facilities where they could gather the ill and prevent diseases from spreading further. The goal was the same: The longer a disease could be restricted to a small group, the better the chance that the disease would run its course without affecting the population at large. Hospitals focused as much on isolating the sick as they did on healing them. Given the primitive conditions of the time, containment was sometimes the only rational option.

Disease has always been a particular danger to the crews of ocean-going ships. Before the steam engine was used to power ships in the 19th century, the only way to traverse the ocean was under sail. The ships generally moved slowly; sometimes they were at sea for months at a time, and the crew lived in close quarters. An outbreak of a contagious disease could incapacitate or kill a majority of the crew, leaving the ship without enough hands to fight or to bring the ship into port. (Recall that the ship that is said to have introduced the plague to Europe at the city of Genoa reached port with a majority of its crew

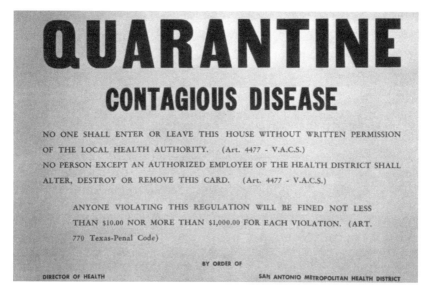

Quarantine sign. Quarantines were once a common method of protecting the public health. Today's public-health officials are more circumspect in their use. [Courtesy of Centers for Disease Control and Prevention]

In this picture, first published in 1884, travelers from Switzerland are kept in quarantine at Bardonnechia, Italy, for five days as a preventive measure against the importation of cholera. [Ann Ronan Picture Library/HIP/The Image Works]

already dead.) On the other hand, the ocean itself served as a barrier to the introduction of new disease. A ship that left port free of disease-causing microbes would remain so—at least until it reached the next port of call.

During the days of sail, entering port was as much a matter of public health as it was of seamanship, and for ships entering a foreign harbor, the maneuver also entailed no small amount of diplomacy. Ports were common entry points for disease, and in those days, many ports maintained at least one boat or small ship to intercept and inspect arriving vessels. Before a ship could drop anchor or tie up to a dock, its captain had to prove to port officials that his crew was healthy. No port master wanted to bear the blame for allowing a potentially devastating illness into his nation, just as no captain wanted his vessel to become known as a plague ship. Because of this mutual desire to avoid the blame for disease, compliance was generally good.

Ships that found themselves with a contagious disease on board had other responsibilities. They had to warn any other vessel that approached about the risk of exposure to the infection. In the days before radio, ships often communicated via signal flags that they hoisted on lines running from their decks to their masts. A ship with sick crewmen or passengers hoisted a yellow pennant, an internationally recognized signal of a ship in quarantine, and stationed an officer or crewman to yell warnings to anyone who came to investigate.

These rules held until well into the 19th century and the transition from sails to steam power. After thousands of years, ships were gaining independence from the whims of the wind. Sea voyages became increasingly predictable, effectively bringing nations closer together. As transit times decreased, there was less time for a disease to run its course before the ship arrived at the next harbor. The number of ships, the quantity of cargo, and the number of passengers were all on the increase. It was clear that the rules for handling shipboard illnesses would have to change.

Seafaring nations such as Great Britain and the United States established hospitals that were dedicated to treating injured and sick maritime sailors; naval sailors usually were treated on board ship or in naval hospitals. ("Naval" usually refers to combat fleets, while "maritime" covers merchant ships as well as private seagoing craft such as yachts and scientific exploration ships.) Rather than forbidding ships from entering ports or confining all their crew and passengers on board, port authorities began to transfer the sick to onshore hospitals for treatment and isolation. Those without disease would be allowed off the ship after a medical exam.

These sailors' hospitals became major sites for infectious disease research and pioneering treatment. Similar work took place in military hospitals. As physicians and scientists learned more about how diseases developed, and as national populations grew, these hospitals and their staffs began having an effect that went far beyond treating sick sailors. In fact, these institutions would become some of the most important centers in the ongoing effort to control infectious microbes.

Training Medical Detectives

As recently as the middle of the 19th century, people blamed infectious disease on causes such as bad air or emotional upset. In her book *Little House on the Prairie*, Laura Ingalls Wilder tells how her family contracted malaria—"fever'n'ague," as they called it—during an infestation of mosquitoes on their farm during the 1860s in Oklahoma Territory. Her family is rescued by a passing physician who treats the family with a bitter, powdered medicine (more than likely, a drug called quinine made from the bark of the cinchona tree) and calls in neighbors to help the Ingalls family recover. These neighbors describe how other families on nearby farms came down with fever'n'ague as well, blaming the disease on eating watermelons that some settlers had grown on the banks of a nearby creek.

But well before Wilder's birth in 1867, the scientific understanding of disease had begun to quickly evolve. Pioneering physicians began

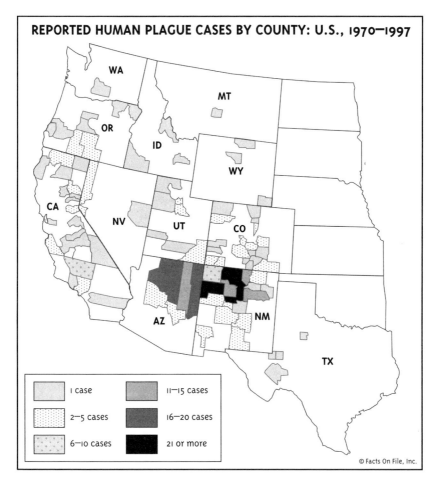

REPORTED HUMAN PLAGUE CASES BY COUNTY: U.S., 1970—1997

1 case		11—15 cases
2—5 cases		16—20 cases
6—10 cases		21 or more

© Facts On File, Inc.

Epidemiologists at the Centers for Disease Control and Prevention continue to monitor the plague, the disease caused by *Yersinia pestis,* which, because it survives in nonhuman reservoirs, remains a potential health threat in the United States, as it does in several other areas of the world.

questioning and changing the accepted principles of medicine around the end of the 18th century. Among the first of these pioneers was Dr. Edward Jenner, an English physician who established the process of vaccination to prevent smallpox. Two facts led him to develop his technique. One was the experience of Lady Mary Wortley Montagu, the wife of England's ambassador to Turkey in 1716, who discovered that the Turks warded off the disease by scratching themselves with a small amount of pus taken from people who had mild cases of smallpox. After a usually mild case of the disease, the people who received the treatment never again developed the disease. The procedure, called variolation, was not without risk. Sometimes the variolated individual developed a full-blown case of smallpox. Sometimes the variolated person infected others with smallpox. Variolation, while often effective, was also controversial because it was so risky.

Jenner sought to modify this procedure to make it safer for all concerned. He was aware of a popular belief that connected milking cows to immunity from smallpox. Farmers and milkmaids sometimes contracted a disease called cowpox from their dairy herds. Cowpox is a pox in the sense that one of the symptoms of the disease was the formation of small pustules, but it is a very mild disease. It is not fatal or even disfiguring. By contrast, smallpox leaves many permanent scars on the survivors. Jenner noticed that those who worked with cows had good complexions— one indication (to Jenner) that immunity to smallpox could be acquired from infection with cowpox. Jenner's hypothesis was that inoculations with cowpox matter would be as effective as variolation and far safer.

In 1796, Jenner decided to put these observations to a scientific test. He took some pus from the hands of a milkmaid and scratched it into the skin of an eight-year-old schoolboy. After the boy's cowpox sores healed, Jenner attempted to infect him with smallpox. The boy did not develop even a mild case of the more serious disease. Soon other physicians began performing Jenner's procedure, which he called vaccination, from *vacca*, the Latin word for cow.

This was one of the first and certainly one of the most important insights into scientific medicine. Here was a safe and extremely effective procedure that prevented a major source of mortality. The discovery depended on real-world observation and experimentation to fight life-threatening maladies. (It is interesting that Jenner's discovery did not depend on the germ theory of disease or any awareness of the mechanics of the human immune response.)

Another victory, one that marked a milestone in public health, took place half a century later in London during a cholera outbreak.

Cholera is a bacterial infection of the intestines that causes massive diarrhea and dehydration. Many cases of cholera occur when the bacterium is ingested by drinking contaminated water. The first person to deduce the mechanism by which cholera is spread was a physician named John Snow (1813–58). Snow had observed some of the effects of the second cholera pandemic, which lasted from 1826 until 1837. The experience left a deep impression on him, and he spent years thinking about the mechanism by which cholera is transmitted.

Although he first published his hypothesis that cholera is transmitted via contaminated drinking water in 1849, his ideas attracted no attention. They were too far out of the mainstream of contemporary thought. When cholera again appeared in England during the third cholera pandemic, which lasted from 1846 until 1863, Snow was anxious to test his theory. He got his chance during a devastating, but highly localized, epidemic in the Broadstreet area of London that began on August 31, 1853. In about 10 days, approximately 500 people died in this small area of the city.

Snow noticed the compact pattern of disease. Investigating the area himself, Snow learned that most of the people in this neighborhood drew their water from the same public water pump. Convinced that the pump water was the source of the neighborhood's high number of cases, Snow asked city officials to remove the pump's handle to prevent people from obtaining water from that source. The officials did not immediately agree to Snow's request because many were skeptical of his theory that cholera could be contracted from contaminated water. There were meetings and discussions, and by the time the pump handle was removed, many of the remaining local residents had already fled and the epidemic was already fading. Consequently the removal of the pump handle failed to provide a convincing demonstration of the correctness of Snow's hypothesis.

A local minister, Henry Whitehead (1825–96), decided to investigate the Broadstreet epidemic further. Whitehead was initially skeptical of Snow's claims, but he did not allow his personal prejudices to affect his analysis. He conducted interviews with family members of those who died as well as cholera survivors. He collected information on where each person lived, the exact time that the symptoms appeared, sanitary conditions, and so forth. The resulting map and Whitehead's analysis were more persuasive, but many still refused to accept Snow's ideas.

In 1866, eight years after Snow's death, there was another cholera outbreak in London. A government worker named William Farr, who was familiar with Snow's ideas, attempted to link the outbreak to drinking supplies. He was successful. He traced the water provided to the area to a pond polluted by sewage. When he shut off this supply of water, the cholera epidemic ended. This provided a final and convincing proof of the correctness of Snow's hypothesis.

Snow and Whitehead had done something new. They had combined medicine with surveys and correlated their data with the local geography to correctly demonstrate the mechanism by which cholera is transmitted. The work of Snow and Whitehead is one of the earliest examples of *epidemiology*, a branch of medicine dealing with patterns of distribution and the control of disease. Epidemiology has since become one of the most effective branches of medicine in the protection of the public health.

In the United States, one of the earliest groups of epidemiologists came from the hospitals that treated sick sailors and ships' passengers. Because ships were such a critical part of commerce and travel, these hospitals had been gathered together under a separate government agency called the Marine Hospital Service, which was organized like a military service. The doctors, nurses, and other staff members already were experts in cataloging diseases and tracing their origins, and the service gradually had taken over most of the nation's maritime quarantine duties. Thus the service was a natural candidate to become a nationwide investigation and disease-prevention agency. Early in the 20th century, Congress changed the Marine Hospital Service to the U.S. Public Health and Marine Hospital Service, later renaming it the Public Health Service and giving it additional duties such as research, food and drug regulation, and medical relief following natural or man-made disasters. As time went on, other health services began taking on similar tasks, particularly in large cities such as New York, which needed such an organization to service its unique and burgeoning population.

Like the federal agency, these other services continued to monitor and treat diseases coming in through seaports, but they also focused on immigrants and visitors coming over the nation's land borders, as well as on epidemics that began solely within the nation. Researchers in these agencies learned how to go beyond the confines of the examination room and track disease organisms to stagnant ponds, colonies of sick animals, ruptured sewage lines, or anywhere else they appeared. After the federal government established the Communicable Disease Center (later renamed the Centers for Disease Control and Prevention) in Atlanta, Georgia, in 1946, the new agency established a more specialized group of medical detectives, the Epidemic Intelligence Service.

These investigators travel within and outside the nation, searching for new strains of infectious disease and looking for ways to prevent them from gaining a foothold in the United States. Other countries have established similar agencies, as has the United Nations' World Health Organization, which provides both medical assistance and research help around the world. These groups form a globe-spanning network that attempts to track and control disease-carrying organisms.

The Development of Isolation Techniques

In order to pursue their work, medical researchers need a way to handle microbes that minimizes the risks to themselves and others. They also need to study these organisms in an environment that does not contaminate the samples with dirt, toxic substances, or other microorganisms. And they have to be sure they neither infect themselves nor allow their specimens to escape. In short, they need a working environment that is safe, sterile, and secure.

What constitutes acceptable levels of safety, sterility, and security has changed as technology has evolved. Modern-day researchers work in labs that meet one of the four biosafety levels. (See chapter 3.) Laboratory standards were much different in the past. The technology was less sophisticated, of course, and less was known about the nature of the microbes being studied. There was also a much greater tolerance for risk. In Edward Jenner's day, the most advanced laboratories of the world were less well equipped than a typical middle-school lab is today. Many scientists conducted experiments in their homes, in backyard sheds, or in rented rooms or buildings.

The primitive and sometimes dangerous conditions under which early researchers labored reflect their budgets and their willingness to risk infection ("experiments" sometimes involved exposing humans, sometimes the researchers themselves, to hazardous microbes in order to prove or disprove a theory). Early safety problems that they sometimes attempted to address involved cleanliness of the lab and the breathability of the air. Labs that were dusty were likely to contaminate chemical reactions or cause unreliable measurements. Ventilation was important because many experiments simply smelled bad, giving off sickening fumes and interfering with scientists' ability to work. To counteract these drawbacks, researchers improvised a variety of devices

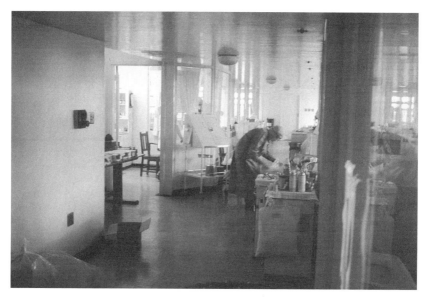

This shows a South African isolation ward during the 1975 outbreak of Marburg virus in Johannesburg. Notice that although the worker wears two masks, goggles, boots, and scrubs, the windows of the unit are open to the outside of the hospital. [Courtesy of Dr. J. Lyle Conrad, Centers for Disease Control and Prevention]

and techniques to isolate themselves from their work. One of these inventions was an eerie-looking isolation garment that looked like a combination of a diving suit and a raincoat. The suit's body was a floor-length rubberized smock that buttoned to the chin, with a pair of rubber gloves that slipped over the close-fitting sleeves. Its crowning feature was a hood that draped over the shoulders, with a pair of goggles stitched into the fabric and a set of breathing tubes that ran down the back of the smock to the floor. These tubes—one for inhaling, one for exhaling—prevented the researcher from inhaling dangerous fumes.

As difficult and awkward to use as it was, gear such as this represents some of the earliest steps toward the "moon suits" in use today. For the most part, though, most medical researchers used less complicated protective equipment in their work, such as surgical masks and operating gowns. Naturally, some researchers contracted the diseases they were studying, and some of these people died. As infectious-disease specialists began to better appreciate the risks that their work entailed, they set about finding better ways to keep microbes from coming into contact with the scientists who studied them.

The efforts that led to the modern-day biosafety laboratories began with studies of how researchers did their work. Design engineers examined how researchers used their equipment, and these studies were used to create workspaces that balanced the researcher's needs for containment with their desire for convenience. Technological developments in other fields found their way into these projects: low-pressure ventilation systems, airtight doors, and self-contained breathing apparatuses—anything that would prevent germs from infecting the researchers. By the middle of the 1960s, most types of biosafety equipment with which we are familiar today were either on the drawing board or in use. From that point on, the tools of infectious-disease research were refined into the forms that researchers use today.

It is also important to note that health-care professionals, when treating individuals with highly contagious diseases, also use many of the technologies that were developed by researchers. As a practical matter, however, containment procedures for an individual infected with a dangerous and highly contagious microbe are more difficult to implement because the microbes are inside the human, and one must be careful to contain the microbes while still respecting the individual. (A sick individual is more than a sickness.) Containment technology in a hospital setting has also taken time to develop: Physicians and nurses must have access to the patient without putting themselves unnecessarily at risk. Furthermore, from a containment perspective, what is in the room must remain in the room; that is, for example, air that is in the room cannot leave until it has been properly filtered. The ability of hospitals to contain infectious microbes is better than it has ever been, but there is still more to be done.

FROM SUCCESS
TO STALEMATE

As culture and technology have evolved, the global human population has burgeoned. Until roughly 1650, it is estimated, the global population never exceeded about 550 million. That maximum is thought to be valid back to the time that the first modern *Homo sapiens* appeared, about 100,000 years ago. Between 1650 and 1850, the population nearly doubled to 1.1 billion. From 1850 to 2000—the period that can be called the era of modern medicine—the number of people in the world rocketed to 6 billion.

Many factors contributed to this extraordinary population boom. Better sanitation systems and cleaner water drastically reduced the incidence of disease. Better agricultural practices and improved means for transporting food made it possible to feed a larger population. Better nutrition ensured a healthier population as well. And, of course, better medicine, especially public-health medicine, limited the incidence and spread of disease.

Not all of these changes were welcome when they were first introduced. Before physicians and health officials could accept advances in medical knowledge, for example, they had to accept that their old ideas about preventing and treating disease were wrong. Beliefs like those that the Ingalls family had about malaria—that the disease came from breathing night air or by eating watermelons that had grown next to a creek—were no more flawed than the views many well-educated physicians held. The most common theories of the late 19th and early 20th centuries still explained illness as an imbalance or corruption of bodily humors, and the most common methods of treating illness involved removing humors from the body. Treatments included drawing blood, inducing patients to vomit, and other, even more drastic, measures. Today physicians usually adapt quickly to advances in medical technology, but it has not always been so.

The Germ Theory of Disease

When he started studying bacteria in the mid-19th century, the French chemist and microbiologist Louis Pasteur (1822–95) was one of the few scientists who believed that microorganisms might be parasites, living within other creatures and plants and occasionally causing disease, but he was not the first to hold these beliefs. The Dutch merchant and microscopist Antoni van Leeuwenhoek (1632–1723) had suggested the same idea when he studied the microscopic world and had used his discoveries in an attempt to disprove the theory of spontaneous generation, the idea that living creatures could suddenly grow out of inanimate materials like soil or decaying plants or animals. But the evidence offered by Leeuwenhoek was not enough to sway the opinion of the majority, including many scientists, who believed that spontaneous generation existed and who pointed, for example, to the appearance of maggots on rotting meat as proof that living creatures could arise out of nonliving substances.

The concept of spontaneous generation was popular and durable for several reasons. First, the idea had been around for thousands of years. The great scholars of the past, including the Greek philosopher Aristotle, had declared spontaneous generation to be a fact. Succeeding generations of physicians and scientists, educated in these ideas, repeated what they had learned. To be fair, the theory of spontaneous generation was not easy to disprove. Without microscopes, for example, there was no way to see either the anatomy of flies or to monitor the day-to-day development of fly eggs into maggots. For many, spontaneous generation seemed the obvious explanation for the available information.

Pasteur, who had access to better microscopes was able to take a closer look at flies and even smaller organisms. He tracked the life cycle of bacteria and protozoa, discovering how they reproduced and how they moved from one site to another. He showed that the theory of spontaneous generation had no basis in reality by proving that microorganisms would not grow in a sample of broth that had been boiled and isolated from the outside air. He became even better known in the 1860s after he saved France's wine industry by identifying bacteria that caused wine to spoil and discovering that gentle heating—a technique that became known as *pasteurization*—could destroy these organisms. A few years later, he performed a similar feat when he developed a way to eliminate germs that were killing France's silkworms. (At the time the production of silk was an important segment of the French economy.)

Soon after these successes, Pasteur published his theory that many of humankind's diseases came from attacks by microbial invaders. By this time, scientists were receptive to the theory, and Pasteur was widely respected as a scientist. He was a careful researcher, and other researchers could reproduce his experimental results. (Reproducibility of experimental results is a key tenet of science.)

Louis Pasteur, French microbiologist and chemist, helped establish the proof of the germ theory of disease and developed a vaccination for rabies. (SSPL/The Image Works)

Pasteur was not the only one to suggest that microscopic organisms cause disease. At about the same time that Pasteur made his discoveries, the German physician and researcher Robert Koch (1843–1910) identified the microbes responsible for anthrax, tuberculosis, and cholera through a long series of creatively planned and meticulously executed experiments. There was, in fact, some competition between Koch and Pasteur. Both, for example, were interested in isolating the microbe responsible for cholera, and when a cholera epidemic occurred in Egypt, both rushed to the scene. Pasteur's team left when one of his assistants contracted cholera. Koch, famous for his precision, was not entirely convinced that the microbe he had found was responsible for the disease. (The epidemic ended before he could be sure of a cause-and-effect relationship.) He later journeyed to the Indian subcontinent, where cholera is endemic, to complete the analysis.

Another example of how deeper insights into microbes saved lives concerns a disease called puerperal fever. In the mid-19th century, a number of physicians began warning their colleagues that they might be responsible for spreading the disease. Puerperal fever is a sometimes fatal, post-childbirth infection of the reproductive system of the mother. The common theory was that the disease was a result of the stress of childbirth, with its accompanying pain and loss of blood. It was thought that there was no way to predict which woman would come down with it, and there was no way to prevent it.

A hypothesis for the basis of the disease was proposed by the German-Hungarian physician Ignaz Phillipp Semmelweis (1818–65), who worked in one of Austria's best-known hospitals, the Vienna General Hospital. The maternity ward of Semmelweis's hospital was divided into two divisions. They were almost identical except that the rate of puerperal fever in one division was three times that of the other division. Only the staff differed from one division to the other.

Semmelweis had the opportunity to investigate the death of an individual who had died from an infected wound at the time that he was investigating the cause of puerperal fever. (Interestingly, Semmelweis's investigations were opposed by his superior at the hospital, who believed them to be a waste of time. The supervisor believed that there was little to be done about the mortality rate in the maternity ward, which was roughly 20 percent.) On close examination, the symptoms of puerperal fever were similar to those of the infection, and he concluded that puerperal fever is itself an infection. He attributed the difference in mortality between the two divisions directly to the staff: The division with the higher mortality trained doctors, while the other division trained midwives. The student doctors were going directly from the dissecting room to the delivery room without washing. When they examined someone who had died of puerperal fever, they simply transferred the disease from the dead person to the individual giving birth. By requiring everyone to wash their hands in an antiseptic solution between examinations, Semmelweis reduced the rate of infection of puerperal fever from almost one in five to about one in 100. Surprisingly, Semmelweis's results initially were highly controversial. Even when presented with the data, many physicians found it difficult to accept Semmelweis's conclusions and what they entailed about past medical practice. In 1861, Semmelweis published his own text on the disease—*The Etiology* [causes], *Concept and Prophylaxis* [prevention] *of Childbirth Fever.* He spent several years defending himself and his work from attacks by his opponents.

Semmelweis died in 1865, but his work was further vindicated later that year. Joseph Lister (1827–1912), a British physician and surgeon, had learned of Pasteur's germ theory and decided to see if he could use it to decrease the number of deaths during and after surgery. He began spraying the air in his operating room with a fine mist of carbolic acid, a harsh chemical he thought would be strong enough to kill microbes without harming his patients. He also washed his surgical instruments in a diluted solution of carbolic acid and required his assistants to wear clean aprons and put on surgical gloves or at least wash their hands. Finally, he forbade any surgeon at his hospital from entering an operating room wearing bloody clothes from previous operations or from reusing instruments without sterilizing them.

These methods dramatically reduced the number of postoperative deaths in the hospital and brought medicine into the era of antiseptic surgery. They also proved that Semmelweis, who had used a milder chemical to kill germs during childbirth, had been correct when he warned that doctors themselves were carrying infections to their patients. The concept of *aseptic* surgery—in which all surgical equipment and the operating room itself are sterilized before surgery—made it even harder for infectious diseases to claim victims on the operating table.

Chemical Weapons against Microbes

Pasteur's germ theory provided another benefit: By exposing microbes as the cause of infectious disease, the discovery finally gave researchers a solid, identifiable enemy to fight. Knowing that infections had a specific cause—one that could be isolated and studied—made it easier for scientists to track down and kill the microbes that had been plaguing humanity. Robert Koch, who, as previously mentioned, was an extremely successful bacteriologist, inadvertently also discovered a way to kill specific germs. In order to see microbes clearly, Koch had learned to dye them. The dye is necessary because without it, he sometimes found himself looking through the microorganisms rather than at them. He discovered that a dye created from coal tar made the organisms visible.

Koch himself did not use the dyes as a medicine. However, Paul Ehrlich (1854–1915), a German bacteriologist, conducted his own experiments with these dyes and found that one, called methylene blue, was able to kill plasmodium, a *protozoan* that causes malaria. Earlier, Ehrlich had discovered that the dye attached itself to and deadened nerve cells, which he thought might make it a useful painkiller for people with severe arthritis. It turned out that the concentration needed to kill nerve cells, even in a direct injection, was strong enough to damage the kidneys. Fortunately, the amount of dye needed to kill the malaria parasite was too low to trigger this side effect. In 1891, Ehrlich gave the dye to two patients who had a mild form of malaria and who responded immediately to the treatment. This experiment was a major breakthrough. It marked the first time that a synthetic drug killed a specific disease organism in patients during an active infection.

Ehrlich's next target was *African trypanosomiasis*, better known as sleeping sickness. Sleeping sickness is caused by a parasite that is transmitted by the bite of an infected tsetse fly. The disease is sometimes fatal and still poses a health risk in certain areas of Africa. Ehrlich and his assistants tested hundreds of substances in an effort to find a procedure for treating someone already infected with the parasite, called a trypanosome, but found none that could kill the parasite without harming the patient.

In 1906, though, Ehrlich learned from a colleague that the trypanosome he was trying to kill was similar to spirochetes, a family of long, thin, spiral bacteria that causes, among other diseases, syphilis. One of the most persistent of sexually transmitted diseases, syphilis is sometimes fatal if left untreated. At the time, there were no effective treatments for the disease. Ehrlich decided to try attacking the syphilis bacteria with a series of arsenic compounds that he had developed in his work on sleeping sickness. One of his assistants, a Japanese scientist named Sacachiro Hata, who joined the lab in 1909, tested the compounds that Ehrlich and his assistants had developed. He achieved suc-

Paul Ehrlich, German bacteriologist and discoverer of
the first effective treatment
for the disease syphilis
[SSPL/The Image Works]

cess with compound number 606, which killed the spirochete without apparent harm to the lab animals it infected. Tests on human volunteers proved that 606 worked, though not without cost. Arsenic, the active ingredient of the drug, is poisonous, and treatments with 606 were painful. Considering the outcome of syphilis, however, most patients willingly suffered through the injections.

Ehrlich named the new drug Salvarsan, a combination of Greek words that means "saved by arsenic." To make sure that Salvarsan saved rather than killed its patients, Ehrlich insisted that physicians give the new drug only to their most seriously ill patients and report the results, especially when toxic effects appeared. Ehrlich kept his own record of each dose on charts inscribed inside the doors of his bookcases. He also insisted on having a sample of each batch of the drug sent to his laboratory so he or his assistants could test it for impurities. Salvarsan was a great success, and Ehrlich's willingness to continue to collect data about drug safety after the release of the drug was both innovative and important.

With this work, Ehrlich founded the science of chemotherapy, the use of chemicals to target specific diseases under scientifically monitored and controlled conditions. Before his work, medications were dispensed on a "best-guess" basis. Some of these medicines were, in fact, effective in alleviating symptoms of a disease, and some helped people return to health. Others did not. Follow-up studies, similar to the one pioneered by Ehrlich, allowed researchers to identify which drugs were most effective for a given use. This enabled researchers to compare drugs, identify improved drugs, and discard the less effective ones.

From Victory to Stalemate

To many in the first half of the 20th century, it appeared as if there would soon be as many effective treatments as there were harmful diseases. It seemed inevitable. The first half of the century saw the discovery of antibiotics, drugs that directly interfere with the life cycle of bacteria and some fungi. First came the sulfonamides or *sulfa drugs* that stopped bacteria from reproducing in the body, thereby providing the immune system with the opportunity to kill the microbes and flush them from the body. Then came penicillin, a drug developed from the *penicillium* mold and discovered by British bacteriologist Sir Alexander Fleming (1881–1955), who noticed that an accidental growth of the mold in a sample dish had killed a large portion of a colony of bacteria he was studying. This discovery led to a worldwide hunt for other forms of mold that secreted chemicals that were equally or more deadly to disease microbes, giving the world the arsenal of antibiotics it has today.

The next great conquest over the microbial world was Salk and Sabin's development of the polio vaccine. More ambitious battles followed. The antibiotic *streptomycin* proved to be an effective weapon against tuberculosis, which had proved resistant to other treatments. Using the insecticide dichlorodiphenyltrichloroethane, or DDT, nations throughout the world began killing the mosquitoes that spread tropical diseases such as yellow fever and malaria. Smallpox vaccinations—much improved since the days of Edward Jenner—had eliminated the deadly disease in North America and Europe. In the 1960s, the World Health Organization began a worldwide vaccination program to wipe out the disease once and for all, and by 1980, the only samples of smallpox still alive were in two government-run laboratories, one in the United States and the other in the Soviet Union.

These public-health breakthroughs received a good deal of public attention; public-health officials and public-health policies were justifiably praised. But among the well-publicized medical victories were some disturbing setbacks. Antibiotics, which people regarded as wonder drugs, turned out to have a vulnerable side: Bacteria were becoming increasingly resistant to their effects.

In every colony of bacteria, some individuals are better able to resist antibiotics than others because in each population there is some genetic variability. One way that the genetic variability manifests itself is through variable rates of survival. If certain bacteria survive a course of antibiotics, they will reproduce and their genes will appear with a higher frequency in the new population. The result is a colony that is more drug-resistant than the original colony. To destroy the new colony, a higher dose of the old antibiotic or a new, more powerful antibiotic may

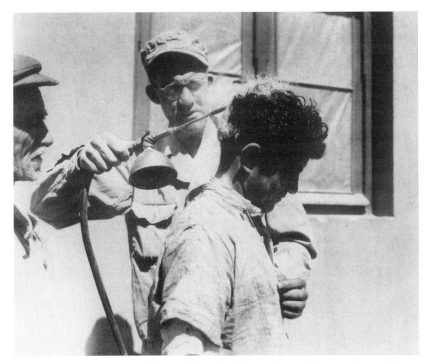

A U.S. soldier demonstrates the use of DDT hand-spraying equipment. The World Health Organization estimates that DDT saved 25 million lives because of its effectiveness against malaria-carrying mosquitoes and typhus-carrying lice. [Courtesy of Centers for Disease Control and Prevention]

be necessary. Drug-resistant bacteria began showing up during World War II, when military doctors began using large amounts of penicillin under poorly controlled conditions. Today there are drug-resistant strains of many types of microbes. There are, for example, variants of the microbe responsible for tuberculosis that are highly resistant to the standard drugs. Because of the deadly nature of TB, this has become a source of real concern among those interested in public health. (This topic is addressed in detail in chapter 13.)

Although a great deal of progress has been made in the last hundred years, the problem of disease has proved to be a more complex one than it seemed shortly after the invention of the first "miracle drugs." Some diseases have yet to be cured, and some that were thought to have been cured are back in new drug-resistant forms. As a result, researchers have been inspired to examine the problem of disease in new and innovative ways.

Scientists have learned to create such microbes: They are deadly and easily transmissible. In some cases, they are also resistant to antibiotics and other medicines. They have created living weapons of mass destruction.

Weaponizing Microbes

Until the middle of the 20th century, disease posed a greater risk to soldiers' lives than combat. Absent any awareness of the role of microbes, the tools and techniques used to treat wounds often introduced infectious organisms into the wounds themselves. Without antibiotics, there was no way to effectively treat infections. Nor was any consideration given to the sanitary conditions under which the soldiers lived, either in camp or on the march. Disease was everywhere.

During war, disease affects both sides, and the attrition is relentless. Over the course of World War I (1914–18), more than 10 million soldiers died from combat over the course of four years. Some scholars, however, give similar estimates for the number of soldiers to have died of the influenza pandemic of 1918–19. While this number is difficult to verify, it is certain that roughly half of all U.S. casualties during World War I were from the flu.

Armies have not simply endured the effects of disease. There have always been those who have sought to use disease as a weapon. Historical records indicate that in 1200 B.C.E. the armies of the Hittite nation, a once-powerful state in the Near East, drove plague victims into enemy territory in hopes of infecting and thereby weakening their foes. In fact, throughout history, many armies have employed a similar strategy. During medieval times, armies besieged walled cities and attempted to destroy those inside by catapulting diseased animal and human bodies over the city walls, and it was via this type of tactic that the Black Death was introduced into Europe (see chapter 5). There are historians who believe that during the American invasion of Canada during the American Revolutionary War, British forces first variolated their own population and then sought to introduce smallpox among the American forces. What is known for certain is that as American forces marched toward Quebec City, a smallpox epidemic erupted and infected half of the 10,000 American troops. The Americans were forced to retreat without further combat, pausing only to bury their dead in mass graves.

Despite the occasional effectiveness of some early bioweapons, most armies have preferred to use more conventional weapons, even during periods of all-out war. Cannons and firearms inflict their damage more quickly. Conventional weapons are also far more accurate, in that disease, once unleashed, can affect one's own forces as easily as those of the enemy.

Scientific progress, however, caused many 20th-century governments to reevaluate the efficacy of "germ warfare." Getting a bacterium to grow in the lab was often fairly easy. Pasteur, Koch, and other 19th-century microbiologists performed this feat repeatedly. Scientists in the late 19th and early 20th centuries, improved these technologies and learned to grow and maintain cultures of a variety of microorganisms—some helpful and some harmful. Once they were able to grow their own cultures under controlled conditions, they became increasingly adept at manipulating these organisms. These advances in microbiology—many made in an effort to save lives—gained the notice of the world's major military powers. Military and political leaders realized that increased control over germs and their properties could lead to a new type of weapon, one based on microbes instead of explosives. All that had to be done was find a way to weaponize microbes, turning them into a form that could easily be launched into and behind enemy lines.

Relief of a Hittite chariot. The Hittites, contemporaries of the ancient Egyptians, engaged in biological warfare. [CM Dixon/HIP/The Image Works]

Fake Treaties
and False Promises

Some of the first victims of this new type of combat were not soldiers but horses. During World War I, horses were still a vital part of military transportation and tactics; in fact, both sides maintained mounted cavalry units throughout the war. To cripple their enemies' cavalry, agents from the German army spread the bacterium *Pseudomonas mallei*, which causes a disease called glanders, among horses and in mules.

In the years following World War I, the major military powers established programs to investigate the potential of bioweapons. Japan, Germany, the United States, and the Soviet Union all initiated bioweapons programs, either before or during World War II. At Camp Detrick (later Fort Detrick), Maryland, American scientists experimented with both human and plant pathogens. The human pathogens were, of course, designed to destroy human beings; the plant pathogens were created to destroy an enemy's food supply. Japan is known to have tested bioweapons on prisoners of war during World War II and to have used the plague, typhoid, and anthrax against Chinese civilian populations.

Bioweapons researchers experimented with increasing the lethality of diseases that were already known to be dangerous. For example, as previously discussed, they worked to increase the lethality of anthrax by altering its spores so that they dispersed more easily. Once inhaled into the lungs, anthrax is usually fatal without quick and aggressive treatment. Smallpox, for which no effective treatment exists, was another topic of research. By producing a strain of the virus for which the standard vaccination was ineffective, for example, one would have a deadly disease that could neither be cured nor prevented.

This type of research is relatively inexpensive, and by the late 1960s, a number of nations, large and small, had established programs to develop bioweapons. Indeed, during the Vietnam War, the United States considered using smallpox on North Vietnamese troops and their Viet Cong allies. The U.S. government eventually rejected the idea as others have rejected it. Bioweapons are simply too blunt an instrument to use strategically. Once the weapons were released, U.S. forces and their allies could have become victims of them as well. Furthermore, when one side uses bioweapons, it invites retaliation in kind. In 1969, President Richard M. Nixon decided to unilaterally eliminate

President Richard Nixon vowed that the United States would not use biological weapons, even if the country itself were subjected to such attack. (PAL/Topham/The Image Works)

all biological armaments in the United States and vowed that America would not use such weapons even if subjected to biological attack itself.

Six years later, the United States, the Soviet Union, and more than 40 other nations signed an international treaty that banned all biological weapons, agreeing not to produce them or store them in their arsenals. Unfortunately, many nations, including the Soviet Union, were violating that treaty even as their representatives signed it. The Soviets continued to develop deadlier versions of their traditional bioweapons and started new projects to create new and even deadlier organisms using *genetic engineering*. By 1989, Soviet scientists had developed several microbes that combined the lethality of some of the world's most dangerous germs and were also easily transmissible.

Despite the secrecy of this work, some news of the Soviet's violations came to light. In 1979, signs of the Soviet violations appeared in the form of a rumored accidental release of weaponized anthrax in Russia that killed at least 1,000 people. Though the Communist superpower denied that anything had happened, a high-ranking defector from the germ weapons program confirmed it, as did information released after the Soviet Union's collapse in the 1990s.

The Threat of Bioterrorism

Military and national-security experts call biological weapons "the poor man's nuclear bombs." Biological armaments are weapons of mass destruction. Rather than affecting a single person or a group of soldiers, as most conventional weapons do, one of these weapons can kill thousands of people. They are relatively easy to deploy; they can even be deployed from the palm of a person's hand.

In 1984, a biological attack was carried out against the community of The Dalles in Wasco County, Oregon. The community hospital and area physicians were overwhelmed by an eventual 750 confirmed cases of gastrointestinal infections caused by a bacterium called *Salmonella typhimurium*, one of the hundreds of types of salmonella that can contaminate food. It was an epidemic of food poisoning, and the scale of the epidemic was extremely unusual. During the previous three years, there had been a relative handful of salmonella cases, less than half of which had been caused by the *typhimurium* strain. Almost all of the cases during the epidemic involved the one strain of salmonella and people who had eaten at restaurant salad bars. And then there was the matter of the timing: The poisonings had occurred in two distinct episodes.

The federal Epidemic Intelligence Service took up the investigation. A team of EIS officers began investigating area restaurants, tracking down the wholesalers and farmers who supplied the restaurants, interviewing restaurant patrons who had become ill, and testing all the ingredients used in both the salad bars and the other items the restaurants served. The only thing that the investigators could confirm was that none of the food had been contaminated before it reached the restaurants. The bacteria had shown up sometime between the time food was prepared in the kitchen and the time it reached the customers' plates. But for years, no one could say for sure how the bacteria reached the food.

Eventually, investigators learned the truth: The food poisonings had been the result of a biological attack carried out by members of a local religious cult who followed an Indian guru, or spiritual teacher, named Bhagwan Shree Rajneesh. These cult members had bought a large ranch in Wasco County in 1981. Their goal was to take over the county government, which was based in The Dalles, and turn Wasco

County into a community ruled by the guru's teachings. The only thing that stood between the cult members and their goal, they believed, was the rest of Wasco County's 20,000 residents, many of whom opposed the cult's plans.

One of the buildings in the tiny town of Rajneeshpuram (they had changed the name of the town in which the ranch was located from Antelope, Oregon) was a sophisticated medical research laboratory, paid for with money donated by the cult members. Here, a few researchers grew salmonella bacteria under orders from the guru's chief assistant, Ma Anand Sheela. Sheela, who actually ran the commune for the reclusive guru, had come up with a plan to make the cult's opponents too sick to vote on election day, ensuring that more votes would go to candidates and issues the cult supported. The September 1984 food poisonings had been a test run of this plan, a limited attack to see if a small group of cult members could contaminate the food and escape undetected.

No one noticed when a few individuals sprinkled bacteria-laden water over the vegetables, in some salad-dressing containers, and in a few jars of coffee creamers in restaurants in and around The Dalles. In fact, no one was able to tie the cult to the attacks until Rajneesh himself, claiming to have been unaware of his follower's plans, told the authorities that his assistant and her small group of associates were the ones responsible. Though county officials suspected the cult was responsible, none of the investigators handling the case could find any evidence directly tying members of the community to the outbreak. It was not until 1985 that investigators learned who within the cult had been responsible and how they had put the elements of the attack together.

The cult's attempt to gain control over Wasco County was the first incidence of bioterrorism in the nation during modern times. This attack showed how vulnerable the nation could be to a well-planned campaign of germ warfare. The laboratory that prepared the salmonella did not contain any equipment that was not available on the open market, yet it had better equipment than that of the Wasco County Health Department. The cult members were able to buy their initial stock of salmonella bacteria from a private germ bank simply by forming a private medical corporation based at the ranch. Distributing the bacteria was simple: The cult members carried it in small vials or spray bottles as they visited their targets.

This was not the only such attack on the United States, nor was it the only one to expose the weakness of the law-enforcement agencies when confronted with this nonconventional crime. The anthrax letters of 2001 created a nationwide panic, yet the person who sent them was still free as of the end of 2005. And, as the U.S. government itself admitted, a bioweapons lab can be as small as a shack in the desert. The admission occurred in 2001 when the *New York Times* revealed that American biowarfare researchers had set up a simulated germ weapons factory on a military base in the Nevada desert, roughly 110 miles from Las Vegas, simply to see how small they could make such a facility. When the news broke, politicians and activists across the nation criticized the government for approving such a project, which seemed to violate international laws and treaties forbidding bioweapons research. But if it was this easy to build a lab, who else might have one?

BIOHAZARDS ABROAD

From the point of view of epidemiology, there are few truly far-off places any more. An epidemic anywhere in the world can pose an imminent risk to the citizens of every nation, no matter how distant. Microbes responsible for a deadly disease on one side of the globe can now find their way to the other side within days. This fact of modern life means each nation's health-care system is often as important to the rest of the world as it is to its own citizens. But although the speed with which pathogens can move about the globe has changed, it has always been true that travelers have had to pack a sense of caution along with their luggage.

The Risks That Travelers Face

Travelers can find themselves in regions where certain microbes are endemic, or native, to that particular region and to which the traveler has no immunity. To protect themselves and others, travelers must prepare for the encounter.

There are numerous examples from history of the dangers posed to newcomers by endemic microbes. The construction of the Panama Canal, which was begun in 1880 by the French company Compagnie Universelle du Canal Interocéanique and completed in 1914 by the

Biological hazard logo. The free flow of people around the world creates great cultural and economic benefits, but it also poses challenges to the public health as travelers are exposed to unfamiliar pathogens and, in turn, sometimes expose others to those same biohazards. (Courtesy of Henry Mathews, Centers for Disease Control and Prevention)

U.S. Isthmanian Canal Commission, provides an especially dramatic example of the hazards posed by disease. The construction of the Panama Canal is often described as one of the great engineering projects in all of human history; it is also one of the great successes in the field of public health. It is no exaggeration to say that the public-health measures undertaken during the construction of the canal made the canal itself possible.

The French company that began the project was unable to complete it. There were several reasons for their failure, but one of the principal ones was disease. To understand the scale of the problem keep in mind that Panama is warm all year long; it rains often and hard for much of the year. (Average rainfall on the Pacific coast is approximately five feet (1.6 m) per year; rain falls at about twice that rate along much of Panama's Atlantic coast.) The interior contains extensive swamps that provide ideal breeding grounds for mosquitoes, and these mosquitoes often carry the microbes responsible for the diseases yellow fever and malaria. When the French began to dig the canal they made little provision for the health of their workers. Under French supervision, 20,000 workers died from yellow fever and malaria. Many more were incapacitated.

When the Compagnie Nouvelle du Canal de Panama, the successor to the first French company to undertake construction, sold its holding to the United States in 1904, the United States established a Sanitary Department headed by experts in the field of tropical diseases. To protect their workers, they radically altered the environment in the area of the construction site, a long, broad region that spanned the Isthmus of

Panama. (The canal is 50.7 miles [81.6 km] long.) They undertook an extensive program of draining wetlands, ponds, and other bodies of water, however small, in order to deprive the mosquitoes of their habitat. When, due to the topography of the land, drainage was not possible, workers poured large quantities of oil into the water to "seal" the surface of the water and so kill the mosquito larvae. If the oil did not have the desired effect, they regularly applied liberal amounts of a custom-made larvicide containing a caustic soda and carbolic acid. They even hired collectors to make daily searches for individual mosquitoes in tents and buildings. The effects were dramatic: Yellow fever, a major source of mortality among the workers during the French episode of construction, was eradicated as a source of mortality. Although malaria proved somewhat more resilient, the program was still highly effective. Deaths among all workers from malaria were reduced from a high of 11.59 per 1,000 in November of 1906 to 1.23 per 1,000 in December of 1909. This extremely aggressive mosquito-control program, undertaken with the aim of controlling the vectors for these two very dangerous diseases, saved tens of thousands of lives.

Locks at Pacific end of Panama Canal. The U.S. construction of this canal was made possible by extremely aggressive and successful attempts to protect the lives of the workers against the pathogens responsible for malaria and yellow fever. (Courtesy of Dr. Edward P. Ewing, Jr., Centers for Disease Control and Prevention)

Not every dangerous or exotic disease is located in a faraway country. There is, for example, an unusual and sometimes fatal lung disease in the American Southwest to which newcomers to the region are particularly susceptible. Called valley fever, the initial symptoms of this disease are similar to those of the flu and pneumonia. It is, in fact, sometimes misdiagnosed as one of these other illnesses. In its most virulent manifestation, the microbe responsible for the disease spreads beyond the lungs and through the bloodstream, where it causes meningitis, an inflammation of the soft tissues around the brain.

The microbe that causes valley fever is a fungus, *Coccidioides immitis*, that lives in the soil of the southwestern United States, particularly in California's San Joaquin Valley and central Arizona. It also grows in northern Mexico and isolated areas of Central and South America. The disease is transmitted through the air when winds or machinery lift the spores off the ground together with the dust in which they are imbedded. The majority of individuals exposed to the fungus display no symptoms. Many others display flu-like symptoms, and a minority of those exposed to *C. immitis* become severely ill when the fungus begins to grow in their lungs, clogging airways and releasing toxins. One infection generally confers lifelong immunity, so many native Southwesterners are already immune to the effects of the fungus. By contrast, newcomers to the area are, as a group, more vulnerable, since, presumably, few of them will have any exposure to *C. immitis*.

Infection rates vary widely from year to year and depend on everything from the weather to construction projects to earthquakes. Whatever agitates the soil increases the rates of infection. Medical treatment for those susceptible to the fungus can be expensive, time-consuming, and debilitating (the drugs used to treat the infection are powerful and have unpleasant side effects), but because the disease is occasionally fatal an aggressive treatment regimen is sometimes necessary. Multiple treatments may be needed, and those who are susceptible to the disease may be sick for weeks or even months. Researchers are currently investigating the possibility of a vaccine.

Biohazard Control around the World

Each region of the world has its own endemic population of bacteria, parasites, viruses, and molds with which those people native to the area

This American Airlines Boeing 777 was quarantined upon arrival at San José International Airport, San José, California, when three passengers exhibited symptoms of SARS. [Norbert Schwerin/The Image Works]

are often familiar and to which their immune systems have sometimes adapted. The risks posed by these organisms are often well understood. Another type of risk occurs when new microbes evolve over very short periods of time. In these cases, the risks associated with these new strains of microorganisms are initially unknown, as is the microbe responsible for the new disease.

Microbes, especially viruses, have, on occasion, evolved fast enough to create new diseases virtually overnight. The SARS outbreak of the early 2000s, which started in China and spread rapidly across the globe, is but one example of this phenomenon. Another is the avian influenza or "bird flu" epidemic of 2003 and 2004, which cost Asian poultry producers from Japan to Pakistan billions of dollars. This variant of an avian flu virus infected 34 people, of whom 23 died, by the end of March 2003.

Influenza viruses are specialized in the sense that each has evolved in such a way that it is capable of infecting only certain types of plants or animals. There is no universal pathogen. Sometimes, however, a variant of the virus can make the jump from one species to another, sometimes adapting to one or more intermediate species along the way.

It is important to understand that most microbes are unable to adapt to other species. Most viruses that affect domestic animals, for example, are unable to infect humans, because (as previously noted) their ancestors adapted to take advantage of particular characteristics of the cells of the species on which they normally prey. But the genetic code of the individual viruses *of the same type* generally differs slightly from individual to individual. These variations may arise from random genetic mutations, or the variations may be the result of the direct exchange of genetic material with other organisms. (It sometimes happens, for example, that viruses exchange genetic material with other viruses or with their hosts.) Sometimes these changes in the virus's genetic code enable the individual virus to infect cells of a new species, and sometimes humans are that new species. The danger associated with this change of host arises because humans have had no opportunity to develop an immune response to the new invader. If the virus is capable of being passed from human to human rather than simply from nonhuman hosts to the humans who care for them, the situation can be extremely serious: Under these conditions the entire human population is simultaneously vulnerable.

This type of phenomenon, medical researchers believe, is how new flu strains develop, including the strains that set off each year's flu season. This explains why new strains of influenza, whether or not they are presently capable of infecting humans, are taken very seriously by those interested in protecting the public health. And if a new and particularly aggressive viral strain infects humans for the first time, health authorities do everything they can to eliminate the strain before it evolves the capability of human-to-human transmission.

A new virus appeared in South Korea in 2003. Chickens and ducks began to show symptoms of an extremely virulent strain of influenza. Affecting only a few farms at first, the strain began spreading throughout huge flocks owned by large chicken-producing corporations in Korea and in other Asian nations. Ducks and wild birds also proved susceptible to the disease. The flu spread quickly, threatening the poultry industry in this region of the world. Health officials knew the strain posed a potentially serious threat to humans as well. The governments of the affected nations ordered producers to kill millions of birds. The massive cull was an effective means of limiting human exposure to the virus, but this approach could not eliminate the new strain. Because the virus is also present in wild birds, it now forms a more or less permanent part of the environment.

Asia has not been the only place to experience such an epidemic. In February 2004, a different strain of bird flu appeared in British Columbia, Canada, and spread to several farms in the province's southwest over a period of two months. By the end of March, more than 365,000 birds at 48 farms within a three-mile quarantine zone had been killed in an attempt to prevent Canada and the rest of North America from suffering the same problems that Asia was facing.

The virus responsible for this form of bird flu is thought capable of rapid evolution into a form that could infect and possibly kill millions of people. Although the disease has spread from bird to person and from person to person, as of early 2005, no strain of the virus has spread easily along either path.

The World Health Organization (WHO), an agency of the United Nations, the CDC, and other national organizations, collects information on newly discovered strains of viruses with the potential to infect humans. Their goal is one of preparedness. Researchers gather as much information as possible about the symptoms caused by the virus, its mechanism of transmission, and the existence of nonhuman reservoirs, and, of course, samples of the virus itself are collected and stored under appropriate levels of security. The information gleaned from this research is used to calculate risk, and if the epidemic is already underway, it is used to determine how fast the epidemic is spreading and how big an area has been affected. These facts are, in turn, used to devise

A 1978 aerial view of the Centers for Disease Control and Prevention (CDC) headquarters in Atlanta, Georgia. The CDC has long been one of the most important centers of its kind in the world. [Courtesy of Centers for Disease Control and Prevention]

possible containment strategies. Data collection and analysis and mathematical modeling are core activities of these organizations. Together these groups form a network that is often the most important line of defense against a new pandemic.

It is sometimes the case that individual nations cannot control the spread of disease because they often cannot exert sufficient control over a wide enough area. WHO serves as a vital source of information for public-health officials and as an apolitical coordinator of emergency services. In the face of a potential pandemic, all nations, rich and poor, large and small, must cooperate to contain the new threat. Resources must be shared. WHO makes such cooperation possible, and historically their record in this regard is quite good. (It was WHO, not any single national government, for example, whose efforts resulted in the eradication of smallpox, and they expect to perform the same feat with polio in the next few years.)

Learning Lessons from the Past

One of the first transnational attempts to control a global pandemic occurred in response to the threat posed by the disease cholera. For most of its history, cholera has been relegated to the Indian subcontinent. In the last 200 years, however, it has spread throughout the globe during a series of pandemics. The second pandemic, which occurred between 1826 and 1837, was the first to reach Europe and the Western Hemisphere. As cholera appeared and reappeared during these years, European researchers theorized that international commerce was transporting the disease. To control the spread of cholera, nations attempted to control commerce and travel across their borders.

In 1851, ambassadors from nations throughout Europe traveled to Paris for a meeting called the International Sanitary Conference, where they began working on how to put such restrictions into effect. The problem was a difficult one to solve, and the first conference ended without any agreement on how to halt the progress of the disease across national borders. Other international conferences followed. Eventually, the nations agreed to a series of requirements for inspecting livestock and other cargo that they believed were potential sources of contamination (recall that they did not understand how cholera is transmitted at this time). They agreed to attempt to prevent people from traveling across borders if they showed signs of severe illness. At the same time, countries throughout the world began forming public-health services and laboratories that focused on fighting the diseases that led to widespread epidemics.

Over the next hundred years or so, medical knowledge improved and spread across the globe, giving nations more tools in the effort to control disease-causing microbes. Most countries required their citizens to be vaccinated against common illnesses before traveling to foreign lands, and they frequently barred visitors from entering unless they had been vaccinated. Regulations were enacted that prevented children from entering public school unless they were inoculated against the most frequent childhood diseases. Quarantine protocols were established for livestock and pets that enabled the destination country to isolate the animals until they were sure that the animals were disease-free.

But quarantines and programs of mass vaccination must be administered judiciously because they require so much in the way of resources, and resources are always finite. To protect a nation from foreign diseases, health authorities must know which diseases pose the greatest danger and in what regions of the globe these microbes are found. This is another reason why national and international health organizations exist: These groups provide policy makers with the expertise necessary to rationally manage risk. Not every safety protocol can be instituted; not every vaccine can or should be administered to the general population. Risk assessment enables thoughtful policy makers to use their limited resources in a way that best protects the public health.

Contemporary methods of monitoring and control cannot guarantee that a potential epidemic will not spread far beyond its point of origin. But contemporary public-health policies and technologies have had remarkable successes. Smallpox was eradicated, SARS was contained, cholera has been largely brought under control. And while some diseases, such as tuberculosis, malaria, and HIV/AIDS, have proved more difficult to control, the successes show that enormous progress has been made and give hope for a healthier, safer future.

11

BIOHAZARD ACCIDENTS AND BIOHAZARD INCIDENTS

Microbes are creatures of chance. They disperse randomly through-out the environment and most will fail to reproduce, but when a germ finds a suitable host it will continue to reproduce as long as con-ditions enable it to do so. A colony of microbes may well reproduce until they kill the host upon which their survival depends, and in this sense, they are predictable: Given the same conditions, they behave the same way. This type of predictability has enabled researchers to create effective safety equipment and safety protocols. Furthermore, because microbes are ruthless—albeit devoid of malice—the failure of safety equipment and safety protocols creates predictable risks to researchers and others.

Needlesticks and Laboratory Slipups

There is no way to treat infectious diseases without coming close to the microbes that cause them. Physicians and nurses face this risk every day, whether they see patients in a private practice or work in the less predictable environment of a hospital emergency room. Researchers who wish to study infectious diseases must also place themselves in an environment close to the germs they wish to understand.

People, of course, make mistakes. Even when dealing with highly lethal microbes, scientists can forget to follow part of a laboratory's containment procedure. When working in the field, researchers can slip and fall into contaminated streams or inhale contaminated dust. And when dealing with patients, the men and women who make healing their profession can suddenly find themselves stricken with the same illness they are trying to cure.

Of all the people who work with infectious diseases, hospital nurses run some of the greatest risks of accidental infection. Even more than physicians, nurses spend their entire working day treating patients on a one-on-one basis, giving them medicine, drawing blood, inserting intravenous drip lines, and performing other tasks that can expose them to any germs their charges may be carrying. Among the most common dangers that nurses face are *sharps*, the term used for needles, scalpels, hypodermic syringes, and other pointed or razor-edged instruments. Sharps are found throughout a hospital, and they are designed to come into contact with blood or other fluids. In the past, hospitals reused many of these instruments, sterilizing them in boiling water and keeping them in germ-free containers until needed. However, the rise of AIDS in the 1980s forced medical researchers to reevaluate these methods, especially as some HIV infections turned out to have come from instruments that supposedly had been sterilized.

These days, most sharps are designed to be used just once and then thrown away. Instead of disposing them in the regular trash, however, hospitals and medical offices use special disposal containers to isolate this refuse. For small items such as syringes or scalpel blades, a typical disposal container is little more than a sturdy, thick-walled plastic box with a trap lid that prevents blades or needles from being removed or accidentally falling out. When full, these containers are either incinerated on-site—as are other types of medical waste—or taken to approved medical-waste disposal sites.

Until they reach these special containers, though, used sharps pose a danger to those who use them. Whenever nurses or doctors use sharps, they have to be on guard against accidentally jabbing themselves or someone else with the instrument. Needlesticks, accidental pokes or scratches with a used syringe or IV needle, are particularly dangerous, as these instruments are designed specifically to inject or

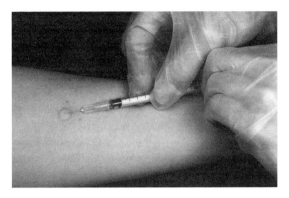

Technician administering a Mantoux tuberculin skin test. The same syringes and other medical instruments that save lives when properly used become health threats themselves when improperly discarded.
(Courtesy of Greg Knobloch, Centers for Disease Control and Prevention)

remove fluid from the body. Any microbes on or inside the needle's hollow shaft may get into the body, where they may start an infection.

Increased awareness of the dangers posed by sharp implements has come at a price. Syringes, which are designed to save lives, have also served to transmit disease. It has long been known, for example, that intravenous drug users who share needles often transmit the virus that causes viral hepatitis, a microbe that damages the liver. HIV, the virus that causes AIDS, can be transmitted the same way. Health professionals who treat individuals infected with viral hepatitis or the HIV virus must take particular care when handling sharp implements, lest the devices that were designed to save lives become vectors for one or both diseases.

Between 1985 and 1999, there were at least 55 confirmed cases of HIV infection and 136 possible cases from needlesticks in the United States, according to the Centers for Disease Control and Prevention. There are, however, 600,000–800,000 needlesticks a year in the United States alone—again, according to the CDC. In fact, a study of worldwide HIV infections from needlesticks revealed that health workers have a 0.3 percent risk of becoming infected with the virus each time they accidentally jab themselves. While the risk of accidental transmission of HIV via accidental needlesticks is low, the HIV virus is so dangerous once contracted that new procedures and regulations continue to receive study in an effort to further reduce the possibility of accidental infection.

When compared with smallpox, however, HIV is a relatively low-risk virus with which to work. A famous and tragic case of accidental exposure to smallpox occurred in 1978 when a British medical photographer named Janet Parker was at work in the anatomy department of the University of Birmingham School of Medicine in England. By this time, the worldwide campaign to wipe out smallpox had almost completed its work. The last natural case of the disease had appeared in Somalia the previous year, and the World Health Organization was just two years away from proclaiming smallpox eradicated from the natural world. On July 25, 1978, medical-school researchers were still studying the smallpox virus in a laboratory that happened to be on the floor below the anatomy department.

This lab had not been designed to provide the type of containment needed to keep the virus from escaping, and an air duct transported air from the lab to the room where Parker was working. As researchers worked with samples of smallpox on the floor below her, some of the viruses were released into air that eventually found its way into Parker's office. About two and a half weeks later, Parker came down with the disease. She died on September 11, 1978, the last person in the world to succumb to smallpox.

Medical Waste on the Shore

Many countries have highly regulated, specialized procedures for the disposal of medical waste. The idea is to safely dispose of the waste so that people are not placed at risk of infection. Burning in carefully monitored incinerators will destroy infectious microbes, but some of the materials that constitute medical waste—such as the plastic used for sharps boxes—release toxic fumes as they burn. An alternative strategy is to bury medical waste at carefully designed sites where the chance they will pose future risks is minimized.

Most of the time medical facilities follow the required procedures to safely rid themselves of their medical waste; they either do all the work themselves or hire specialized medical-waste disposal companies. These services handle incineration, delivery to disposal sites, government-required documentation, and the other procedures involved in the task. In the past, however, the system has occasionally broken down and infectious waste found its way into the surrounding environment. Most of these mishaps are the result of simple accidents or inattention. Someone on the staff, for example, may inadvertently mix medical waste with nonhazardous waste.

Sometimes, however, the "mistakes" are a matter of policy, usually stemming from a desire to cut costs or increase profits. At times, medical facilities ranging from big-city hospitals to small-town clinics have been caught simply tossing away infectious waste as through it were ordinary trash. Some disposal companies have done much the same thing, disposing of medical waste at regular landfills rather than the more expensive special-use facilities. Sometimes medical waste has simply been dumped in out-of-the-way sites in the hope that no one will discover the crime.

One of the most notorious incidents of mishandling took place in 1988. That summer, tons of garbage washed up on beaches along the East Coast of the United States. Most of this garbage was normal household and office refuse, but there was also some medical waste—syringes, blood vials, and other contaminated equipment—mixed in. Though most of the garbage was not infectious, the idea of used needles sticking out of the ground and puncturing beachgoers' feet repulsed the public.

Fortunately, no one was seriously injured in this incident. There was enough of a public uproar, however, for Congress to pass the Medical

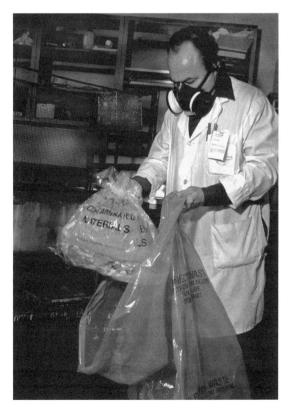

Hospital technician disposes of hazardous waste. Lapses in safe disposal protocols can be hazardous to the public health. [Marty Heitner/The Image Works]

Waste Tracking Act of 1988, which attempted to create a federally managed system to regulate medical-waste disposal. The 1988 law was a first step, and the waste-tracking program had a limited effect. Only New York, New Jersey, Connecticut, Rhode Island, and Puerto Rico took part in the project; a larger, nationwide program never came about, and Congress did not renew the act when it expired in the early 1990s. By that time, the furor over the 1988 incident had faded from the public memory.

The incident and the act that followed it had one long-lasting effect, however: Until the 1988 incident, medical-waste disposal was governed by a mix of city, county, and state regulations that sometimes presented contradictory standards. During the early 1990s, state governments tightened the rules for disposing of potentially infectious rubbish, setting standards that hospitals, medical schools, and other facilities use today.

Creating New Diseases by Accident

In the laboratory, new disease may arise by accident or by design. Understanding how experiments go right and how they might go wrong is an important step toward protecting the public health.

Since the early 1970s, researchers and industrial scientists have attempted to use the techniques of genetic engineering to alter bacteria to create pharmaceuticals and to harness benign viruses to repair faulty genes. One of the first successful uses of genetic engineering, in fact, was to alter the bacterium *Escherichia coli* to produce insulin, a hormone that helps control how the body uses sugar. First discovered in 1921, insulin is produced in the pancreas, which secretes the hormone directly into the bloodstream. Sometimes the body fails to produce enough insulin, leading to a condition called diabetes. Insulin injections can compensate for this deficit.

Early attempts at producing insulin involved filtering it from the pancreases of cattle or hogs. Today most insulin comes from *E. coli* bacteria whose genes have been augmented with human insulin-making genes. Drug makers grow the engineered bacteria in huge vats, and the bacteria produce insulin as they grow and multiply. This method for producing insulin, which has been in use since the 1980s, is more efficient that the earlier method.

The remarkable results obtained by applying the concepts and techniques of genetic engineering to medicine have encouraged scientists to seek new areas in which to apply these ideas. In particular, a group of scientists in Australia during the late 1990s decided to apply genetic-engineering methods to one of the nation's biggest problems: mouse control. In the process of attempting to alter the genome of a mouse-specific pathogen, they produced a new type of organism that demonstrated how this kind of experiment could go wrong.

Rodent infestations are a major issue in Australia, where "plagues" of mice regularly destroy large quantities of grain—an important part of the Australian economy. The scientists, who worked at the Cooperative Research Center for the Biological Control of Pest Animals in Canberra, decided to alter the virus that causes mousepox—a member of the same family as smallpox and monkeypox—and turn it into a contraceptive microbe. They spliced enough mouse genes into the virus for it to reproduce the chemical signature of a mouse egg on its surface, then injected the virus into a female mouse. As the mouse's immune system developed antibodies to the virus, the scientists thought, it also would develop antibodies that would attack the mouse's own eggs.

At first the plan worked well. The altered virus triggered the hoped-for response, effectively sterilizing 70 percent of a test group of mice, but two other test populations, which were made up of two different breeds, were not affected. To boost the virus's sterilizing power, the scientists inserted another gene into the virus's genome. This time the new gene was one that would cause the virus to produce a protein called interleukin-4, which increases the number of antibodies that the immune system produces. Since the protein occurs naturally in mice, the scientists thought the second alteration would simply accelerate the sought-after effect.

They were wrong. The introduced interleukin-4 gene disabled part of the immune system that responds to viral infections. Even though the researchers had chosen a mild strain of mousepox on which to conduct their tests, all the mice injected with the doubly altered strain died within nine days. Further, altering the previously mild virus had made it extremely resistant to pox vaccines. They had created a form of mousepox against which their vaccine was ineffective. Even when mice were inoculated against the pox, the altered version was lethal 60 percent of the time.

None of the scientists involved in the project had intended to create a virus with this property, but their accidental discovery had profound

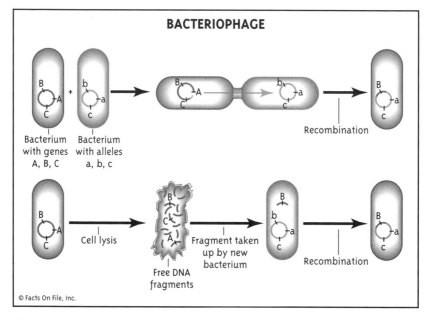

The processes of conjugation and transformation are two ways that bacteria can exchange genes without human intervention.

implications: Mousepox is similar to smallpox, and there is a human form of interleukin-4. A similar modification of the smallpox genome could conceivably produce a smallpox virus that is resistant to the small-pox vaccine. Their work pointed to the possibility of creating a virus against which standard vaccinations would be ineffective. Furthermore, there is no apparent reason why the same sorts of techniques employed by the Australian team could not be employed by others to produce still other types of microbes against which standard treatments would be ineffective.

It is important to recognize that the manipulations scientists purposely perform in the laboratory can also happen at random in nature. It does not take computerized gene-splicing equipment to shift fragments of DNA from one microbe to another; bacteria and viruses are capable of gene swapping without human interference. A lethal pathogen with the same properties that the Australian researchers pieced together in their laboratory might arise spontaneously. The challenge for those interested in protecting the public health, then, is to create an infrastructure of highly skilled workers capable of identifying new types of potentially dangerous microbes and to find ways to protect the public against new pathogens. This must be accomplished at a speed that enables them to react quickly enough to minimize the effects of the microbe on the public health.

THE RISE OF WORLDWIDE PATHOGENS

Different types of microbes affect the same host in different ways. Some microbes, such as cholera, overwhelm their host quickly. Other disease organisms, such as HIV, work far more slowly. Methods of transmission also differ: Some microbes are transmitted through casual contact; some are not. Sometimes contact is not required at all. The microbe responsible for TB is inhaled; once the TB pathogen is in the air, we can no more avoid it than we can avoid breathing. Other diseases are spread in a far more complicated fashion. West Nile virus spread quickly throughout much of North America because it infected migratory birds. Mosquitoes carried the virus from the bodies of birds to the bodies of a variety of mammals, including humans. The basic principle of evolution applies to all microbes: The individuals belonging to a given species of microbe that produce more viable offspring will have their genes better represented in the next generation. In this way, gene frequencies change over time, and every type of organism evolves.

To be more exact: The physical properties of an organism are the raw material upon which evolutionary processes operate. Different combinations of physical traits are more or less conducive to evolutionary success *in a given environment*, where success is always measured in

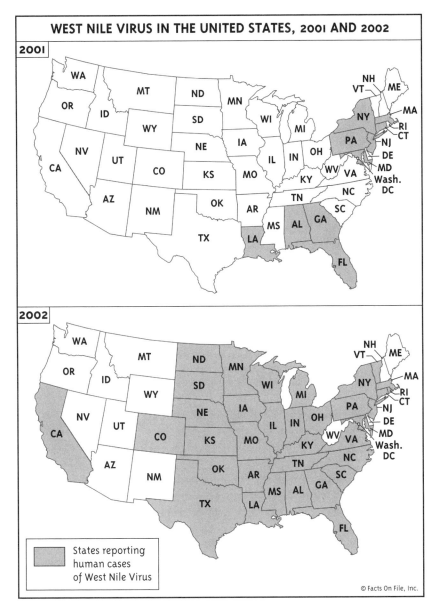

WEST NILE VIRUS IN THE UNITED STATES, 2001 AND 2002

Map showing which states reported incidences of human infection by West Nile virus in 2001 and 2002. Because of its effectiveness in exploiting its nonhuman hosts, West Nile virus spread quickly throughout the United States.

terms of how many viable offspring are left by the individual. In other words, it is the interaction of the particular organism with the environment in which it finds itself that determines evolutionary success. For example, some bacteria are more resistant to antibiotics than others; some are more resistant to ultraviolet rays. No combination of traits is always superior to another. Evolutionary success depends on the physical traits of the organism *and* on the environment in which the organism finds itself, and insofar as these physical traits are determined by the genetic inheritance of the organism, differential levels of evolutionary success lead to changes in gene frequencies in the next generation. Evolutionary processes act on the genes indirectly and only so far as the genes determine the physical characteristics of the organism.

These general statements about evolution apply to all living organisms. In the case of higher organisms, genetic change generally occurs as the frequencies of certain genes in the population vary from one generation to the next; that is, for higher organisms genetic change (evolution) occurs *between* generations. Microbe gene frequencies are also altered in this way, but many microbes have evolved in such a way that they are also able to change their genetic structure immediately. Viruses sometimes incorporate small pieces of their hosts' DNA into their own genome, and certain bacteria have been observed exchanging genetic material with other bacteria. This additional mechanism of genetic change enables microbes to change their own genetic structure almost instantly. This has important implications for public health.

Frequent changes in gene frequencies and genetic diversity create the potential for new and potentially hazardous microbes to arise quickly and without warning. The rate at which dangerous microbes are created is difficult to determine, since a newly discovered pathogen is not the same as a newly created pathogen and distinguishing between the two is not always easy. It is sobering, nonetheless, to consider that some of the world's most virulent diseases are, at least, newly discovered.

Ebola and Marburg

At first the patients exhibit no more than a headache or a slight cough. A day or two later they start running a slight fever, they feel tired, they develop aching muscles and joints. Soon their temperature rises. They develop severe diarrhea, which leads to dehydration. Then comes the bleeding: from the nose, from the gums, from every other orifice in the body, including the edges of the eyes. Delirium follows. The disease is often fatal.

Hemorrhagic fevers (the word *hemorrhagic* means that one of the principal symptoms of the disease is bleeding) are the product of viruses that attack and destroy blood vessels, interfere with the blood's ability to clot, and prevent the kidneys from functioning correctly, causing a buildup of dead cells and other particles in the blood. In many forms of hemorrhagic fever, bleeding alone is enough to kill the infected individual, especially if there is bleeding into the lungs. Those who do not die from these diseases—and some have death rates of up to 90 percent—can be permanently disabled with kidney injuries, breathing problems, and other ailments.

Ebola is one type of hemorrhagic fever. The first known cases of the disease appeared in the Ebola River region of northwestern Zaire (now called the Democratic Republic of Congo) in 1976. There is no known cure. It can kill people within a week or two after the first symptoms appear, but it is not thought to pose a danger to the population at large. Because Ebola is so deadly and so quick, the victims often die before the microbe responsible for the disease can be transmitted to a new host. The biggest single outbreak of Ebola took place in Kikwit, in the Democratic Republic of Congo, where the disease killed 250 people in 1995.

Historically, researchers have had only limited success in tracking the origin of these most virulent of microbes. In the late 1960s, for example, a form of hemorrhagic fever appeared in the German cities of Marburg and Frankfurt, and in Belgrade, Yugoslavia. Most of the 31 people who came down with the disease were part of the medical industry. The first Marburg patients worked or were related to workers at a pharmaceutical plant; the first Frankfurt patients worked in a pathology research lab; the Belgrade victims were a veterinarian and his wife. The disease infected families, coworkers, and physicians who tried to treat the first patients. Before long, the hospitals that treated the victims placed them in highly secure isolation wards to protect their own staff. About half of the people who came down with the disease died; the survivors experienced permanent organ damage.

No one had ever seen cases quite like these, and at first no one understood the way that people in such widely separated cities could have developed the same illness. The Marburg and Frankfurt cases had one element in common, however: The first victims worked in research labs where they conducted experiments using vervets, also known as African green monkeys, imported from Uganda. But there did not seem to be an immediate connection with the case in Belgrade—until researchers from the World Health Organization began tracking the monkeys' journey to Europe.

The investigators discovered that the monkeys belonged to three groups that had been shipped from Uganda to Belgrade. Each group reached Yugoslavia with an unusually high number of losses—half of the first shipment of 99 vervets arrived dead. The rest were quarantined until a local veterinarian could examine the bodies and determine if the others were infectious. Even though the dead monkeys showed signs of unusual bleeding, the veterinarian determined that the other monkeys were safe to transport and allowed them to continue their trip to Germany. It was that veterinarian and his wife who developed the disease that also struck the laboratory workers.

With this knowledge, researchers began to search for the primary source of the disease, which had been named Marburg hemorrhagic fever, after the city in which the first cases were identified. Researchers looked in West Africa for the reservoir of the virus. This is especially important, since it is believed that the primary transmission pattern of the virus is from its natural nonhuman reservoir to humans. The human-to-human route of virus transmission is thought to be secondary. The reservoir of the virus remains unidentified.

Research has shown, however, that in sub-Saharan Africa, Marburg hemorrhagic fever is both rare and lethal. This makes it difficult to understand. In particular, patterns of transmission and the risk factors involved are poorly understood. (The disease strikes quickly and there are few survivors left to interview.) Instead, researchers undertake *antibody* surveys, wherein they test the blood of different segments of the population for the presence of specific antibodies. When a person is exposed to a microbe, the immune system forms antibodies, specialized cells specific to that microbe, in order to destroy the foreign organism. For each microbe to which we are exposed, our blood carries an antibody created to destroy it. Some of these antibodies remain in our bloodstream long after the pathogen has been destroyed. In effect, our blood carries a history of the microbes that invaded our bodies. (This record is more comprehensive than simply the microbes that made us sick. If we are exposed to a dead or weakened microorganism our body will still form the antibodies necessary to destroy it even though we may never exhibit any of the symptoms of the disease caused by healthier versions of the same microbe. This is the idea behind vaccination.) What the researchers discovered is that less than 2 percent of all those tested carried an antibody for the Marburg virus. This disease remains poorly understood.

large quantities of hantavirus. As the urine dried, it turned into a powder that easily floated into the air. Because human habitats also make good rodent habitats—with plenty of food, water, and places to hide—colonies of the rodents can be found near homes, so there is plenty of opportunity to breathe in virus-laden dust.

The scientists were less clear about how the hantavirus had made its way into the United States. Korea had been open to world trade for decades before the discovery of the new disease. Shipping certainly carried rats and mice between Korea and America, as well as between Korea and Europe, where other strains of hantavirus have been found. Perhaps these rodents were the vectors. Once the virus reached the American coast, it found its way into native rodents and spread, later evolving into its lung-damaging form. The American form of the virus cannot be passed from person to person but can only be contracted by breathing in the pathogen. The disease, which is now called hantavirus pulmonary syndrome, has no cure. Treatment includes medication to keep the airways open and oxygen administered through breathing tubes or in oxygen tents, but survival depends on whether or not patients can stay alive until the disease runs its course.

The Rapid Adaptations of HIV

AIDS was identified as a separate infectious disease in the early 1980s, but the disease had been around for years before physicians recognized it for what it was. Because it had such a long *latency period*—the time it takes for a microbe to trigger the symptoms with which it is associated—the human immunodeficiency virus could not have developed later than the mid-1970s. More than likely, researchers thought, a similar virus had existed for decades, if not centuries, in animals but had only recently made the jump to human beings. In order to understand the nature of the disease, they began to search for the origins of HIV, the virus that causes AIDS.

Beginning in the 1950s, health services throughout the world began to keep tissue samples from patients who had died from unusual, unidentifiable illnesses. Researchers looked through these old cases to see if any showed the same symptoms as those of modern AIDS cases. They found several cases of people who died with symptoms of what would now be called AIDS; analysis of these tissues revealed ancestral forms of the virus that is now known as HIV. The earliest example of HIV infection was identified in a blood sample from a man who had lived in Kinshasa, the capital of the modern-day Democratic Republic of Congo, in 1959.

Another clue to AIDS's origins came from the animal kingdom. AIDS researchers reasoned that the virus could not have developed solely within human hosts; it had to have had its start in an animal that lived close to, or even among, human beings. In their quest to find HIV's origins, scientists analyzed blood and tissue samples from apes and monkeys living in Africa, Asia, and South America. They discovered a virus they called SIV—simian immunodeficiency virus—that had some similarities to HIV. The two viruses were similar enough to warrant further investigation. The scientists uncovered several lines of evidence, all of which pointed to the idea that HIV is a human variant of SIV.

First, analysis of HIV has shown that there are actually two types of HIV: HIV-1, the strain of virus that causes AIDS throughout the world, and HIV-2, which seems mainly to strike victims living in Africa. Some of the primate samples contained a strain of SIV with a genetic code suspiciously close to that of HIV-1. Furthermore, the strain was living within the bodies of chimpanzees, which, of all the great apes, have a genetic code most similar to that of humanity's.

Second, people in this region hunted primates for food. Killing and preparing an animal for consumption involves many opportunities for exposure to any pathogens that the animal might be carrying.

The transformation of SIV into HIV, the scientists believed, might have gone this way: During the 1940s or early 1950s, chimps began carrying a form of SIV that could survive in the humans who hunted them. Given a strain of SIV that could infect humans, it was only a matter of time before a primate infected with that strain was killed and prepared as food. One or more of the individuals then became infected with SIV, and as the virus evolved in its new (human) environment, a new type of virus, the human immunodeficiency virus (HIV), emerged. From those hunting parties, HIV has spread throughout the globe.

HIV infects human immune cells in a manner that is similar to the way that SIV affects primate immune cells. Both viruses carry "keys" on their outer shells that allow them to break through cell walls of certain cells associated with the immune system. At the same time, the viruses prevent the immune system from identifying them as hostile intruders by frequently changing their surface appearance, making it all but impossible for healthy immune cells to produce antibodies that will be effective against the virus. Like a spy adopting new disguises and forging new identification papers, HIV is able to dodge the immune system long enough to infect more cells and switch identities yet again.

By itself, HIV is a fragile microbe. It cannot survive more than a brief exposure to the open air, and many household cleansers and disinfectants can kill it. Consequently it is extremely unlikely that it will be transmitted through any type of casual contact. Nor can it be transmitted through the air. The only way HIV can be transmitted between individuals is when bodily fluids containing the virus are exchanged. Such an exchange, usually in the form of blood or semen, enables the virus to pass from one individual to the next without exposure to the outer environment.

Despite the special conditions required for transmission of the virus, it can now be found throughout the world, and in many nations it is a principal cause of mortality among young adults. In Botswana in 2003, approximately 37 percent of all pregnant women carried HIV, and in several African countries, average life expectancy has dropped precipitously because of HIV/AIDS after rising steadily for decades. In other regions of the world, infection rates are lower but still quite significant, and public-health authorities struggle to find creative ways to contain the disease and to treat those already infected.

Health authorities in several countries have adopted policies that have proven effective in containing the spread of the HIV virus. Among these policies are educational programs that inform those who are sexually active about ways to minimize the risk of becoming infected. Needle-exchange programs and educational programs help reduce the practice of sharing needles among intravenous drug users. Sensitive tests have been devised for donated blood; these enable hospitals to be confident that they will not transmit the virus during a blood transfusion or organ transplant. Finally, various drugs have been created, and others are in the testing stages, that often enable those with the virus to maintain an active, relatively healthy, lifestyle indefinitely. The situation is far better than it once was, but much remains to be done.

DRUG RESISTANCE

Evolution is the process by which gene frequencies change from one generation to the next. The changes can occur quickly—new frequencies can arise over only a few generations—or they can occur very slowly. Scientists have found honeybees trapped in amber, a kind of fossilized tree resin, that were alive more than 65 million years ago during the time of the dinosaurs. They appear to be structurally identical to some modern species of tropical honeybees, indicating a very slow rate of evolution.

When scientists attempt to estimate the speed with which various species of organisms are capable of evolving—note that it is the species of organism, not the individual organism that undergoes the process of evolution—one important factor to consider is the length of a generation. Recall from chapter 12 that gene frequencies change as individuals produce offspring. If an individual produces no offspring, then that organism's genes are not represented in the next generation. But if an organism produces many offspring (and other organisms of the same species produce relatively few) then the genes of the more prolific organism will be more common in the next generation.

For higher organisms, a generation is the average length of time that passes between the birth of the parents and the birth of the offspring. An analogous definition for microbes would be the average length of time that passes between reproductive cycles. Generation

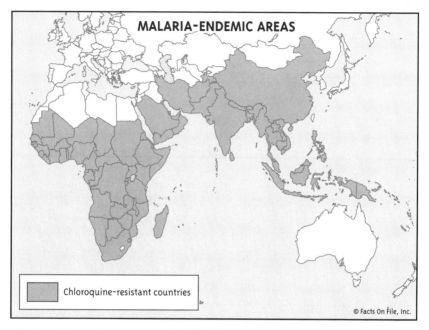

MALARIA-ENDEMIC AREAS

Chloroquine-resistant countries

© Facts On File, Inc.

The drug chloroquine was once a highly effective treatment for malaria, but it is no longer as effective as it once was. Chloroquine-resistant strains of the malarial parasite have evolved in many widely separated regions of the world.

times vary widely among living creatures. If we assume an average human generation of about 15 years (for most of human history people began reproducing almost as soon as they were able), then roughly 350 generations separate us from those Sumerians who created the first written language 5,000 years ago. By contrast, a species of bacterium that reproduces roughly twice each hour—and these types of bacteria exist—will have undergone almost 88 million generations during the same 5,000-year period. Because gene frequencies change between generations, a species with a very short generational period will have the potential (all other things being equal) of evolving faster than a species with a longer generational cycle.

But the rate at which evolution occurs depends on several characteristics of the species; it is not a simple matter of the average length of a generation. Another important characteristic of a species is the amount of variability in the physical and behavioral characteristics of the individuals. The sum of all physical and behavioral characteristics of an individual is called the *phenotype* of the organism. If all individuals of a species are identical—in appearance, in behavior, in resistance to disease, etc., that is, if they have identical phenotypes—then given identical circumstances, the reproductive outcomes will also be identical. Each individual would behave precisely as every other individual, and, as a consequence, in the same environment all members of the species would produce the same number of offspring. Essentially, if we think of the environment as a sort of test, all members of this hypothetical species would pass or fail the test together. In order for a species to evolve, there must be variation in the characteristics of the individual members of a species.

Finally, not all variation is significant from the point of view of the scientist interested in evolution. In order for an individual trait to have an effect on the future of the species, it must be possible for that individual's offspring to inherit that trait. Not all traits can be inherited. For example, if a person carries a scar as the result of an injury, that scar cannot be inherited by that individual's offspring. Scars are, it is true, a type of individual variation, but because they cannot be inherited, they have no evolutionary significance. Only variations in an individual phenotype that stem from individual variations in our genes are significant from the point of view of evolution. The sum of our genetic inheritance is called our *genotype*. From an evolutionary point of view, variations in the phenotype of an organism are significant only insofar as the phenotype represents the genotype. Environmental processes act on the phenotype, and in doing so they affect which genotypes will be present in the next generation and which genotypes will be eliminated—or at least see their frequencies reduced. The evolutionary process consists of "weeding out" certain genotypes and allowing others to survive. In the next generation, the remaining genotypes recombine to produce still other combinations, and then these, too, are "tested" by the environment—some are passed, some are eliminated, and the process is repeated once again. Evolutionary processes are almost as old as the planet upon which we live.

By human standards, human evolution is too slow to observe directly. In order for a new trait to become prominent or for a once-common trait to become rare, many generations must pass. As a consequence, it is unlikely that any of us will survive long enough to notice changes in the human phenotype that result from evolutionary processes. The fossil record proves that such changes occur, but it also indicates that they occur over the span of many generations; they are far too slow to observe directly. In the case of microbes, the situation is entirely different. Microbes reproduce so quickly and there are so many of them—and there are so many different phenotypes on which the environment can act—that we can easily observe them evolve. In fact, human intervention has had important effects on the course of microbial evolution.

Acute Otitis Media

Acute otitis media (AOM) is the ear infection that is so familiar to parents of young children. The symptoms include inflammation (redness) of the middle ear and a bulging membrane inside the ear called a tympanic membrane, or eardrum. The disease often arises as the result of a cold. A cold, which is caused by a virus, causes tissue in the eustachian tube, which connects the ear to the throat, to swell slightly. In children, the eustachian tube is narrow, and the mild swelling caused by the viral infection also causes the eustachian tube to close. Fluids begin to collect between the eardrum and the point at which the tube has pinched shut. Bacteria multiply in this warm, wet environment; the immune system attempts to destroy the foreign bacteria. Pressure in the ear increases, and the result is pain. Children, especially very young children, respond to the pain by pulling on the infected ear. This continual pulling and tugging is an important symptom of AOM, and often the first question a pediatrician will ask a parent is whether the parent has observed the child tugging on his or her ear. The pain is often severe enough to make it impossible for the child to sleep or play normally. The microbes responsible for AOM hardly qualify as biohazards—they are not dangerous enough—but the processes that have affected the genetics of these nuisance organisms are often identical to those that have affected the genetic codes of more hazardous organisms. The difference is that AOM is common; we can observe the phenomenon directly. As individuals, we may even have contributed to it.

Although the infection is usually not visible without special equipment, parents quickly become aware of the possible presence of AOM because their children cry continually. The onset of AOM is generally rapid, and a child that is happy and alert one day may well be distracted and in pain the next. In the United States, ear infections are the most common infection in children for which antibiotics are prescribed. In the year 2000, some 16 million children were brought to doctor's offices for treatment of AOM. Approximately 82 percent of those children were sent home with a prescription for antibiotics to treat the bacterial infection inside the eustachian tube. A course of drug therapy generally costs between $10 and $100. Taken together with the costs of the office visit, the cost of treating routine ear infections in the United States runs into the billions of dollars each year.

In recent years, however, physicians and researchers have noticed a hidden biological cost to the routine treatment of AOM with antibiotics. The bacteria responsible for AOM are becoming increasingly resistant to the medicines used to destroy them. Tests have shown that in 30 percent of the cases involving *Streptococcus pneumoniae*, the most common pathogen involved in AOM, the bacterium is now somewhat resistant to penicillin, and, in fact, in half of all cases involving resistant *S. pneumoniae*, the bacterium is classified as highly resistant to penicillin.

It is not hard to see how resistance to penicillin might arise. In the United States, antibiotics are used to cure AOM in many millions of cases each year. That means that physicians have used penicillin to cure ear infections hundreds of millions of times since the drug's introduction. When it was first introduced, penicillin was described as a miracle of modern medicine, but there is nothing miraculous about it: Penicillin and the class of drugs related to penicillin destroy bacte-

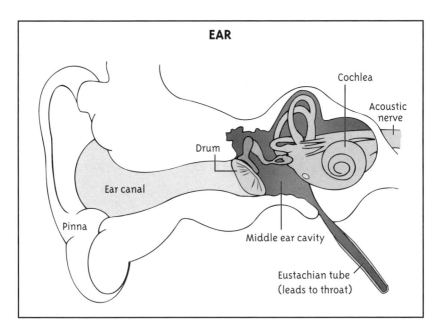

When the narrow eustachian tube is pinched shut, infection of the region behind the ear drum and above the pinched region can occur.

ria by acting against the cell walls of the pathogen. It is remarkably effective, but there have always been a few bacteria that were more resistant than others. Some of these resistant bacteria produce proteins that disrupt the structure of penicillin before it can do its work. Others have cell walls that lack "receptors," spots on the cell wall where the penicillin molecule can attach itself. Penicillin-resistant bacteria are more likely to survive an encounter with penicillin than other bacteria, and as a consequence, they are more likely to be found in an environment where there is plenty of penicillin than their non-resistant counterparts, and that is exactly the environment in which they find themselves. Furthermore, in a population of penicillin-resistant bacteria, some will be even more resistant than others. The frequent use of penicillin causes the frequency of genes present in these bacterial species to shift toward gene complexes that make the carriers ever more resistant to penicillin.

This evolution of *S. pneumoniae* toward strains that are increasingly resistant to penicillin and similar drugs is also related to how the drugs are administered. In order to be effective penicillin must be administered regularly over the course of several days (usually a 10-day course of the drug is prescribed). By continually exposing the bacteria to a hostile penicillin-rich environment for a prolonged period of time, the microbes are usually destroyed. Even bacteria that are somewhat penicillin-resistant will eventually succumb to the effects of the drug. Ideally, this is how the drug should be administered, but in reality parents sometimes forget doses or stop administering the drug before the 10-day period is over. The reason is that their child seems healthy again. The symptoms have disappeared; the crying has stopped. But stopping early sometimes means that only the bacteria that were particularly susceptible to the drug have been destroyed. Other bacteria that were resistant remain. Stopping the drug too early means that the infection may return, and this time the eustachian tube will be occupied by the offspring of the resistant bacteria. This is evolution at work.

In the last several years, American physicians have begun to change how they treat AOM. They have become increasingly willing to follow the lead of their European counterparts. In western Europe, physicians tend to treat the symptoms, especially the pain of the ear infection, rather than the cause. Instead of antibiotics, they prescribe pain relievers and then observe the child for a period of 48 or 72 hours. It is frequently the case that the child's own immune system will, if given the extra time, rally and control the infection without the help of antibiotics. Of course, the strategy of "letting nature take its course" will not always work, but usually it does. In the United Kingdom, a comparison of the two methods of treatment showed that if no antibiotics were initially administered, 76 percent of the children recovered on their own. (Antibiotics can, after all, be administered later.) The advantage of this approach is that there are far fewer opportunities for the bacteria to develop resistance to the antibiotic. The drawback of not using antibiotics is that it takes longer to recover. Of the group that did not use antibiotics, 70 percent were better in three days. By contrast, 86 percent of those treated with antibiotics were better in three days.

Parents and physicians have important responsibilities in the wise use of penicillin and other antibacterial and *antiviral* drugs. The overuse of drugs quickly leads to their ineffectiveness. A course of drugs must be administered exactly as prescribed. It is, in a sense, a race against time. Bacteria eventually become resistant to the drugs used to control them, but given enough time new classes of drugs can be discovered and put into use. It is everyone's responsibility to use these medicines wisely.

Hospitals and Germs

Selection pressures are what scientists call those factors that lead to differential mortality. Among humans, for example, each disease is a selection pressure. There is no disease to which all humans are equally susceptible. Even in the case of the HIV virus, some people succumb to the disease far faster than others, and a few manage to live indefinitely with the virus without showing any of the symptoms of AIDS. When the source of this resistance is particular genes or complexes of genes, then the resistance can be inherited. And if the disease remains a significant source of mortality from one generation to the next, one would expect to see the frequency of those genes that confer resistance to rise rapidly.

In fact, in any population of organisms, human or not, the rate at which gene frequencies change depends on the severity of the selection pressures and the amount of genetic variability present in the population. If there is a source of mortality that routinely destroys a large fraction of the population generation after generation (and the remaining organisms survive because of a genetic trait), gene frequencies can shift radically over the course of only a few generations. One might see a previously rare trait quickly become common throughout the population. The speed with which evolution occurs often depends on the environment: The higher the mortality, the faster advantageous genes spread throughout the population.

For microbes, there is no more hostile place than a hospital. One of the main goals of a hospital is to kill germs. People arrive at hospitals infected with a wide variety of pathogens, and these institutions exist, in part, to destroy the germs and prevent their transmission to the staff and other patients. Operating rooms must be kept as germ-free as possible. Surfaces are washed with special chemicals to destroy as many microbes as possible; surgical implements are placed in autoclaves designed to sterilize—to destroy all microbes—and, of course, soap is everywhere: Doctors and nurses must be careful to wash regularly so that they do not become vectors for disease; floors, walls, bedding, gowns, and curtains are all washed regularly.

Despite the best efforts of hospital staff, germs are found in abundance in every hospital. Many pathogens are introduced from the outside as sick individuals come in for treatment, and many more find their way into the institution on the shoes or clothing of staff and visitors. Almost all of these germs are eventually destroyed in an environment that is designed to be as hostile to their presence as modern technology will allow, but a few survive. The colonies of the survivors are regularly decimated by chemicals and drugs designed to destroy them. As a consequence, any genetic variations that allow them to endure quickly become established throughout the colony. Some of these microbes are exquisitely adapted to life in a hospital, and, in fact, some are found nowhere else. They are the so-called superbugs, microbes resistant to some or all antibiotics.

The problem of acquired resistance is an extremely serious problem. In Great Britain, for example, a new class of infection-control positions was created in 2003 by the National Health Service. Every hospital is now required to hire a senior administrator as "director of infection control." Each infection-control director creates and manages teams to investigate and control the transfer of microbes. The problem is acute: Thousands die every year in the United Kingdom from hospital-acquired infections and perhaps as many as 100,000 patients acquire an illness during the course of their hospitalization.

These hospital-dwelling microbes survive due to a variety of factors. One important factor is the reluctance that some doctors and nurses have shown toward adopting such simple procedures as washing their hands between visiting individual patients. Failure to wash one's hands under these circumstances facilitates the transfer of germs from one patient to the next. For the staff, such germs are often hard to identify because they usually do not make the staff ill. Often the main victims are those with open wounds or depressed immune systems. Each newly infected individual is another environment in which bacteria can multiply and is a new case requiring the application of antibiotics. It is a remarkable fact that strains of *Staphylococcus aureus* resistant to the drug methicillin, for example, appeared only two years after the drug was first introduced in 1961.

Furthermore, not only do gene frequencies change in response to the application of antibiotics, but research has shown that whole new genes can appear in a non–drug resistant strain overnight. Researchers had an opportunity to actually find a patient in which an extremely resistant strain appeared virtually overnight. In 2003, the journal *Science* reported that a diabetes patient in Detroit developed foot ulcers, and while in the hospital, these ulcers had become infected with staphylococcus bacteria. Tests showed that while some of the bacteria were resistant to common antibiotics, others showed resistance to vancomycin, one of the most powerful antibiotics available and considered by some to be the last line of defense against highly resistant bacteria. The fact that only some of the staphylococcus bacteria were resistant to vancomycin indicated that a gene mutation had occurred within this particular patient.

Researchers at the Centers for Disease Control and Prevention discovered that another common bacterium, *Enterococcus faecalis*, had exchanged genes with the staphylococcus bacteria, including one gene that conferred resistance to vancomycin. Genes were moving back and forth between entirely different types of bacteria, producing a great deal of genetic variability on which the mechanisms of evolution could operate to produce highly resistant strains in very short periods of time. The situation was considered so dangerous that all of the approximately 300 people who had come into contact with the infected individual were tested for the presence of the highly resistant form of the staphylococcus bacteria. All tests were negative.

In humanity's determination to destroy infectious germs, we have created new and increasingly drug-resistant microbes. The hardiest of these germs live in hospitals and are responsible for thousands of deaths each year. The challenge to health workers and researchers is to create a hospital environment that is hostile to germs and that evolves as fast as the germs themselves. It is a kind of competition between

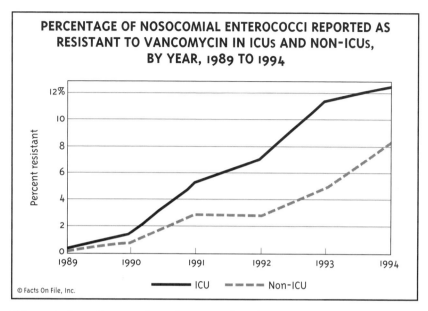

PERCENTAGE OF NOSOCOMIAL ENTEROCOCCI REPORTED AS RESISTANT TO VANCOMYCIN IN ICUs AND NON-ICUs, BY YEAR, 1989 TO 1994

© Facts On File, Inc.

This graph shows the percentage of vancomycin-resistant enerterococci, a type of microorganism, in ICUs and non-ICUs from 1989 until 1994. [The word *nosocomial* means "originating in a hospital."] [Courtesy of Centers for Disease Control and Prevention]

humans and bacteria in which we should all have an interest. The results are a matter of life and death.

Tuberculosis

Tuberculosis, caused by the bacterium *Mycobacterium tuberculosis*, is one of the most widespread of all human pathogens. One-third of the entire population of the world, approximately 2 billion people, is infected with the TB bacillus. Every second of every day, someone becomes infected with *M. tuberculosis*. Ordinarily, someone infected with TB shows no symptoms. Instead, the bacterium enters a dormant phase; it survives inside a (human) cell called a macrophage, whose function is to destroy invading microbes. Only 5–10 percent of those infected with the TB pathogen become sick.

Among those who become sick, lesions develop on the lungs. Left untreated, the lungs become scarred and the patient finds it increasingly

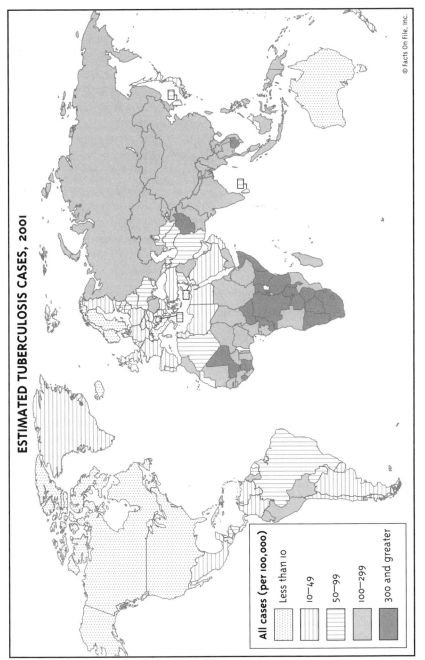

ESTIMATED TUBERCULOSIS CASES, 2001

© Facts On File, Inc.

All cases (per 100,000)
Less than 10
10—49
50—99
100—299
300 and greater

Tuberculosis continues to affect millions throughout the world.

difficult to breathe. The more damaged the lungs become, the less efficiently they function. In 2002, approximately 2 million people around the world died from the disease.

Only those who show symptoms of the disease can transmit the microbe that causes TB. Whenever an infectious person sneezes or even talks, they release TB pathogens into the air. Only a small number of such microbes need to be inhaled to transmit the disease to the next person. According to the World Health Organization (WHO), an individual ill with tuberculosis will, if left untreated, infect 10–15 additional persons over the course of a year.

Throughout the 18th and 19th centuries, tuberculosis was the leading cause of death throughout Europe and North America. As living standards improved in these regions, the incidence of tuberculosis dropped rapidly, and when drugs were first developed to treat TB, it looked as if the disease would cease to be a health threat. These drugs, developed 40–60 years ago, are still used today. They are inexpensive—a six-month course costs about $10—and they are often effective. But they are no longer as effective as they once were. The problem, again, is that TB bacteria have evolved and are sometimes highly resistant to the standard treatments.

The problem of drug resistance here is intimately related to the length of the course of treatment: A six-month course of drugs, while inexpensive, is often difficult to administer. Patients who seek treatment because they are suffering from the effects of the disease soon feel much better. But they are still infected. The symptoms are gone, but those bacteria that were most resistant to the effects of the drugs are still present in the patient's body. If a patient stops taking the drugs—and many patients do—the infection returns. The difference, of course, is that the individual pathogens comprising the new population of disease-causing bacteria are descendants of those drug-resistant individuals from the first infection. As a consequence, they are more likely to be drug-resistant themselves.

In recent years, a type of tuberculosis called MDR-TB, multidrug-resistant TB, has emerged that is resistant to the two most powerful anti-TB drugs, isoniazid and rifampin. MDR-TB is particularly common in the former Soviet Union and poses a global health threat. WHO estimates that 300,000 people contract MDR-TB each year. For those who live in countries without a strong health-care system, the condition is often fatal. Even for those who live in countries where they have access to good health care, the individual who contracts MDR-TB may be quarantined for extensive periods and be subjected to a course of chemotherapy that can last up to two years, a course of treatment that carries its own health risks.

There is no prospect of bringing tuberculosis under control in the near term. In addition to the problem of drug resistance, another contributing factor to tuberculosis deaths is HIV. TB often occurs in tandem with HIV, and worldwide, approximately 13 percent of all those with AIDS die from TB. War and the persecution of ethnic and religious groups contribute to higher rates of disease. The United Nations High Commissioner for Refugees (UNHCR) estimates that in 2003 there were 20 million refugees worldwide. The conditions in refugee camps are often very difficult: The camps are often crowded, unsanitary, and lacking in food. TB thrives in these often temporary camps, and when the population disperses, people carry the disease with them. (Treating TB in the camps is difficult because treatment is long term, and the residents are often short term.)

The evolution of drug-resistant microbes affects developing countries as well as developed ones. In the developed world, it is easy to forget how much we depend on the availability of reliable, fast-acting medicines to cure a wide variety of infections. For many of us, these medicines have been in use since before we were born. That they might cease to function is a very serious health problem. It is, in fact, a certainty that the longer they are used, the less effective they will be. It is the hope of everyone concerned that by using these drugs responsibly, the day that they cease to work will be delayed until substitutes can be found.

PART 4

The Perception
of Disease

MICROBES ON THE MOLECULAR LEVEL

A disease is a many-faceted phenomenon. As scientists, physicians, and the general public have learned to perceive disease in different ways, they have become more adept at understanding and controlling it. A particular disease may, for example, be perceived as a collection of symptoms: The disease in question causes fever or does not; it causes a rash or does not; it causes difficulty in breathing or does not; it causes death or does not. The identification of a disease as a set of symptoms was probably the first way that humans learned to perceive what we now call disease.

Understanding diseases as symptoms has never been more important than it is today, but there are now, broadly speaking, two other ways of perceiving disease. The first is from an epidemiologic viewpoint—when diseases are studied as part of the larger environment. Epidemiologists are interested in disease as an ecological phenomenon. They investigate the mechanisms involved in transmitting disease from individual to individual, and they are interested in the way that organisms responsible for disease exist in the environment, even when they are not infecting anyone. The first successful epidemiological study of disease was John Snow's analysis of cholera in the middle of the 19th century. Beginning in the latter half of the 19th century with the work of Louis Pasteur and Robert Koch, scientists began to study the nature of disease at ever-smaller levels of organization. Koch was interested in identifying the individual microbe responsible for a particular disease. As technology improved, scientists were able to investigate smaller parts of the individual microbe. Today scientists are able to study individual genes. For example, in 2000, the specific sequence of genes that comprises the organism responsible for cholera was first decoded. The study of the molecular properties, including the identification of key gene sequences, of specific disease-causing organisms cannot replace older approaches to disease. But these insights, too, have occasionally proved useful in understanding the nature of disease, and they have, on occasion, enhanced our ability to control disease as well.

Gene Sequencing and Molecular Biology

To understand microbes at their smallest level of organization, the molecular level, scientists have had to devise strategies that depend heavily on technology. Technology is important to researchers because without the help of machines the volume of detail with which these scientists must be concerned would be overwhelming.

Consider the problem of gene sequencing. The molecular "blueprint" for an organism—that is, the information necessary to construct and organize the proteins used in the creation of an organism—is stored in that organism's DNA. (Some viruses have no DNA. Their information is stored on a molecule called RNA, a molecule that is similar but not identical to DNA.) A microorganism's DNA is often organized into a single, extremely long, string-like molecule consisting of functional units called genes. Each gene determines a protein. Organisms of the same type generally have the same genes. Each gene consists of a string of "bases." Determining the order of the bases is the problem of gene sequencing.

From the point of view of the sequencer, each base is represented by a letter. No matter whether an organism uses DNA or RNA as the molecule of heredity, only four letters are used to represent hereditary information because only four bases are used in the construction of the gene. One can think of a gene as a word and the bases as the letters that

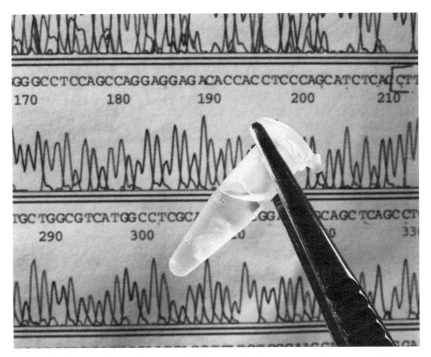

A sample of DNA and a small segment of a map of a human gene. Sequencing techniques are now routinely applied to a wide variety of organisms. [SSPL/The Image Works]

determine the word. The details of the structure of the protein that is represented by a particular gene can be determined by the order in which the bases appear.

Viruses tend to have a very simple genome. Phi-X 174, a virus that preys on *E. coli* bacteria, for example, has 10 genes. By contrast, *Yersinia pestis*, the pathogen responsible for plague, has 4,042 genes; *Mycobacterium tuberculosis*, the pathogen responsible for tuberculosis, has 3,959 genes; and *Vibrio cholerae*, the pathogen responsible for cholera, has 3,890 genes. One gene generally requires hundreds or even thousands of bases (letters) for its expression. In just the same way that changing the order of letters in a word changes the meaning of the word, reordering the bases that comprise a gene changes the nature of the protein determined by the gene. Inheritable variations between individual organisms of the same type are due to variations in the order in which the bases appear in the gene. There is so much detail in the genome of even a "simple" single-celled organism that determining the number of genes an organism possesses and the order of the bases that comprise each gene can only be done by machine.

Decoding the genome of an organism is, however, only the first step. The next step is to discover what the genes mean. This can be done with a *gene chip*. A gene chip is ordered like a small chessboard. The genome of an organism is disassembled, and each individual gene is copied many times. On each square on the board, many copies of a single gene are deposited, and then the array is exposed to different conditions and the researcher observes which squares (which genes) are activated. This enables the researcher to identify which genes are responsible for which individual cellular actions.

These techniques have been used, for example, to study the so-called Spanish flu of 1918, which killed tens of millions of people worldwide. To understand what made the flu so dangerous, researchers needed a sample. They began obtaining samples from graves in the far north—Alaska was one such place—where bodies, buried in permafrost, were sufficiently preserved to contain tissue samples full of the virus that had killed them. The virus was no longer active, but it, too, was well-enough preserved to enable scientists to use sequencing techniques to determine its genome. Armed with this knowledge, they set about determining which genes were responsible for which aspects of the virus's "behavior." They were, of course, trying to determine why this particular virus was so much deadlier than other flu viruses.

Under extremely high security, U.S. researchers created a new type of virus to test their theories. They began with samples of the virus that caused the 1918 pandemic. They had sequenced the genome of this virus and identified two genes that they believed played a key role in the infectious properties of this strain of influenza. Next they took a virus that they knew had no effect on mice. Into the genome of the harmless virus they inserted the two genes that they believed caused the 1918 virus to be so virulent. When the mice were exposed to the hybrid, their lungs hemorrhaged and they quickly died—an experiment described in an article in the journal *Nature* in 2004.

In this case, two genes are the difference between a virus that is harmless to mice and a pathogen that is deadly to them. This experiment is a good indicator of how easily a new pandemic can arise—all it takes is for two genes to be exchanged between two different viruses—and how important it is to better understand the nature of these pathogens.

The Specificity of Viruses

How are viruses able to specialize? Why, for example, do viruses that affect one species of animal not simultaneously affect all species of animals? Why, in the experiment described in the previous section, did two genes make all the difference?

To appreciate the nature of the problem, it is important to understand that viruses are extremely simple microbes. They are so simple that many researchers do not classify them as living creatures at all. Viruses require no oxygen because they do not breath. They require no food because they do not eat. In fact, viruses have very few of the properties that most people associate with living creatures. The one trait that they share with all living creatures, however, is that they reproduce. Unlike other creatures, however, they cannot reproduce without the help of a host.

Structurally, a virus consists of a genome housed in a protective cover. A common analogy is that of a knife in a sheath. This sheath also has molecules called hemagglutinins (HAs) attached to its surface. HAs enable the virus to attach itself to the surface of the type of cell upon which it preys. Each type of cell has receptors on its surface, and each type of virus has its own HAs. These HAs enable the virus to attach itself to particular types of receptors. The HA and the receptor are analogous to a hand and a glove. With this analogy in mind it is easy to see why each type of virus can only attack a particular type of cell. Without a compatible receptor, the virus cannot bind to the cell, and if it cannot bind to the cell, it cannot infect it.

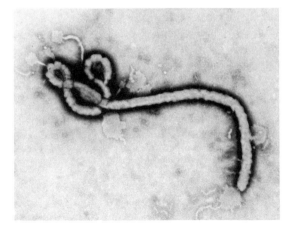

Ebola virus. Every virus is adapted to prey upon certain species of organisms, but in the case of Ebola, it is not even certain in which species the virus normally resides. (Courtesy of Fredrick A. Murphy, Centers for Disease Control and Prevention)

But HAs are no different than any other viral trait. The shape of each HA—and so its specificity—is entirely determined by the genes of the virus. That is how the researchers described in the preceding section knew which genes from the 1918 virus to insert into a virus that they knew to be harmless to mice. They chose those particular genes because they knew that those genes affected the shape of the HAs. By altering the shape of the HAs, they created an entirely new virus, one that could infect the mouse cells. Because the virus was new, the mice had no resistance to it. Before their immune systems could adapt to the new pathogen, they died.

Now it is easy to see how the 1918 virus arose. Researchers believed that the 1918 virus was originally adapted to birds rather than humans. The reason that it suddenly was able to infect humans is that it had somehow made the transition from a highly infectious bird virus to a highly infectious human one. To test their hypothesis they examined the 1918 virus using a technique called X-ray crystallography. This technique entails focusing a carefully controlled beam of X-rays on the virus and recording the way that the proteins on the virus's surface scatter the beam. With X-ray crystallography, they computed a three-dimensional portrait of the shape of the HA. What the researchers discovered is that the HA of the 1918 virus, the HA that enabled the virus to infect humans, was only a small modification of the HA found on some bird viruses. In effect, the bird pathogen was already almost a human pathogen. Only a slight change in the genome of the bird virus was enough to change the shape of the HA and enable it to bind to receptors on human cells.

How did the change arise? No one can know for sure, but it might have arisen as a random error. Viruses reproduce so often that occasionally mistakes are made in the process of reproducing the genome. The sequence of bases that comprise a gene is, occasionally, not an exact duplicate of that found in the preceding generation. The changes are random and so many of these changes produce a virus that is less infectious. But because the changes are random, any mutation is possible. The more complex the change, the less likely it is to occur over the short run, but given enough time, the right combinations of individual mutations is bound to occur.

When that small change occurred in the virus genome that enabled its HAs to bind with receptors on human cells, the microbe was suddenly faced with an entirely new species on which to prey: It had made the jump from birds to people. In 1918, the global human population was approximately 2 billion; by the time the pandemic was over, approximately 1 billion had become infected. Because humans had no prior experience with the disease, no one had immunity. The entire population was simultaneously vulnerable, and the result was a loss of life greater than that caused by the Black Plague.

The Mechanics of Resistance

Faced with an environment filled with many different types of dangerous microbes, higher organisms evolved a variety of ways to defend themselves. The self-defense system that has evolved is called the immune system. In humans the immune system is an astonishingly complex array of responses that enables the body to recognize foreign bodies and often destroy them. Sometimes the microbes are destroyed before they enter the body. If the microbe successfully evades the body's outer defenses and enters the body, other strategies come into play that can destroy the microbe before it enters a cell. If the microbe successfully enters a cell, still other strategies are employed to destroy the microbe inside the cell. But as effective as the immune system is, it could do better. Scientists have learned how to intervene directly to assist our immune system in warding off the pathogens responsible for disease.

The body's first defense system is often described as "nonspecific," that is, the barrier that it creates is not directed at a particular organism but is effective against many different types of pathogens. At its simplest level, it is a simple physical barrier between our interiors and our exteriors. To appreciate the extent of this barrier, it helps to keep in mind how extensive it is. It is easy to see that skin and some of the secretions that form on our skin—certain oils, for instance—protect us from microbes. (The oils contain acids that are harmful to certain bacteria.) But our respiratory system, including the surface of our lungs, also forms an interface between our interiors and the exterior world. This system, too, must be as impervious as possible to foreign matter. For example, the respiratory system secretes mucus to trap foreign particles. Finally, the lining of our digestive system also forms a mechanical barrier between our interiors and the outside world, and this lining, too, is coated with a type of mucus that is harmful to certain pathogens.

If a microbe is able to evade this physical barrier, it encounters a collection of cells whose purpose it is to identify foreign bodies and destroy them. Some of these cells are nonspecific, meaning that they are not targeted against one particular type of microbe but will instead

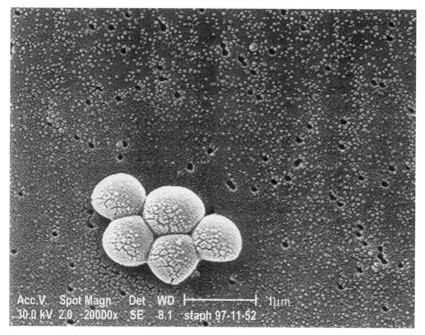

One way that bacteria become resistant to certain antibiotics is to increase the thickness of their cell walls. These *Staphylococcus aureus* bacteria are methicillin-resistant and vancomycin-resistant. The increase in cell-wall material appears as clumps on the surface of the microbe. [Courtesy of Janice Carr, Centers for Disease Control and Prevention]

target anything that they recognize as foreign. These attacking cells are called scavenger cells and natural killer cells. The scavenger cells scour the body, ingesting foreign microbes. There are two main types of scavenger cells: granulocytes and macrophages. Both are nonspecific in the sense that they are attracted by chemical signals and will attack a wide variety of foreign bodies. The natural killer cells attack the body's own cells when they have become cancerous or infected by a virus. They bind to the cell they attack and inject material through the cell wall that causes the cell to rupture and die.

Of particular interest to the study of biohazards, however, are those aspects of the immune system that are specific to particular microbes. That the human body could—if given enough time—adapt to pathogens has been known for a very long time. The Greek historian Thucydides (ca. 460 B.C.E.–ca. 404 B.C.E.) wrote a moving account about an extremely virulent plague that affected Athens in his *History of the Peloponnesian War*. He describes the breakdown of the social order and the widespread death, the sadness experienced by those who were just beginning to experience the initial symptoms and understood their fate, and the suffering of those who remained to care for friends and family fully understanding the risks. He wrote, "Yet it was with those who had recovered from the disease that the sick and the dying found most compassion. These knew what it was from experience, and had now no fear for themselves, *for the same man was never attacked twice—never, at least, fatally.*"[1] (Italics added for emphasis.)

This adaptive aspect of the immune system, what is often called "specific" or "acquired" immunity, is now frequently exploited by researchers to create vaccines. The cells that can adapt to specific microbes are called lymphocytes. Lymphocytes are divided into two main types: B cells and T cells. What these two types of cells have in common is the ability to identify microbes by the three-dimensional patterns formed by atoms on the surface of the microbe. These three-dimensional structures are called *antigens*. They can be very complex. From the point of view of the immune system, the antigen is a marker that identifies the microbe in a way that facilitates an immune response. B cells and T cells have receptors on their surface. A receptor "fits" or binds to an antigen in a lock-and-key or hand-and-glove sort of way; they match. Of course, not every hand fits every glove, nor does every key fit every lock, and not every receptor can bind with every antigen, but the mechanism by which lymphocytes are created enables the body to produce many tens of million of distinct receptor types. (There are an estimated 2 trillion lymphocytes in an average adult.) Furthermore, a complex antigen may bind with more than one receptor.

Once a lymphocyte has bound with an antigen, an immune response may be generated. An immune response means that the lymphocyte begins to form clones of itself, that is, other lymphocytes of the same type and with the same receptors are created. But recall that there are two main types of lymphocytes: The B cells, once stimulated, produce large numbers of antibodies, proteins that can bind with the antigen that stimulated the parent B cell. By binding with the antigen, they are able to chemically disable it. B cells act on pathogens that are in the blood or other bodily fluids but outside cells. Once inside a cell, the pathogen is out of reach of B cells and the antibodies they produce. By contrast, T cells act on pathogens that have already invaded specific cells. They recognize foreign molecules on the surface of infected cells and bind to the cell. These reactions by the B cells and T cells are extremely specific because they are based on very specific molecules.

Once an immune response is triggered, the body is flooded with cells that are able to destroy or disable very specific types of microbes.

Until the 20th century, little was known about the mechanics of the immune system, but that did not prevent scientists from making use of it. The most famous example of this occurred in 1796, when Edward Jenner developed a smallpox vaccine. In modern terminology, the antigen on the cowpox microbe was similar enough to that of the smallpox antigen to elicit an immune response that enabled the body to resist all future infections by smallpox and cowpox microbes. Jenner had learned to elicit the immune response to smallpox without exposing his patients to the smallpox disease. In 1885, Louis Pasteur exposed a boy bitten by a rabid dog to a weakened form of the rabies virus. The virus had been processed—keep in mind that Pasteur did not know what a virus was—so that it was no longer infectious, but it still retained its characteristic antigen. By injecting the boy with the weakened virus, Pasteur was enable to elicit the immune response from the boy's body in time to protect him from the ravages of rabies.

Vaccination is now one of the most reliable methods of disease prevention. Vaccines have been used to prevent some of history's most deadly diseases, and most infants are routinely inoculated for a wide variety of diseases that were once significant causes of mortality. The strength of the technique of vaccination is its specificity. By harnessing the body's own immune system, the vaccination procedure enables the body to effectively resist the microbe that causes the disease of interest. Specificity is, in a sense, also the weakness of the procedure. The often-made observation that there is no cure for the common cold still holds true. There are no vaccines for the common cold, and the reason is that the common cold is a collection of symptoms. Virtually everyone has had a cold, but any number of microbes might be responsible for a particular case of the disease. Furthermore, the viruses themselves continue to evolve, and as they evolve so do their characteristic antigens. As a consequence, there is no efficient way to protect the public from the many different viruses responsible for this disease. Vaccinations are important, but like every technique, they have significant limitations.

[1] Thucydides. "History of the Peloponnesian War." Translated by Richard Crawley. The Internet Classics Archive. Available online. URL: http://classics.mit.edu.

MICROBES AS SETS
OF SYMPTOMS

Microbes have long been identified by the diseases that they cause, but diseases are not the same as microbes. Diseases are sets of symptoms. It is an important distinction to keep in mind: Microbes *cause* symptoms; symptoms are the *effects* of the body's infection by microbes. In this sense, the microbes are more fundamental than the symptoms with which they are generally associated, but most people care little about microbes because it is the symptoms of a disease, not the microbes that cause them, that they notice.

The relationships that exist between microbes and symptoms are often complex and fascinating. The search for new, sometimes subtle statistical connections between the microscopic causes of disease and their macroscopic effects occupies much of the attention of researchers throughout the world today.

Identifying Microbes from the Symptoms That They Cause

A runny nose, sore throat, sneezing, swelling of the sinuses, and, sometimes, coughing are symptoms of the disease called the common cold.

Symptoms generally begin two or three days after exposure and continue for one or two weeks. The disease is rarely serious.

The number of colds one has each year depends very much on one's age. Children generally have from six to 10 colds per year. As a general rule, the older one becomes, the fewer colds per year one has. People over the age of 60 average less than one cold per year.

All of the preceding statements describe a cold as if it was one phenomenon, and from the point of view of the sick person, the cold *is* one disease. But according to the United States National Institute of Allergy and Infectious Diseases, of the National Institutes of Health, the set of symptoms called "the common cold" can be caused by more than 200 distinct viruses. Among the most common causative microbes are the rhinoviruses—so far more than 110 different types of rhinovirus have been identified—and several types of coronavirus. Other viruses that are sometimes responsible for other, more serious diseases may also cause 10–15 percent of all adult colds. Influenza, for example, is sometimes diagnosed as the common cold. Finally, between 30 and 50 percent of all adult colds have yet to be associated with any particular virus.

The common cold and its causative viruses is one instance of a many-to-one phenomenon: Because many distinct causes produce the same effect, knowing only the effect (the symptoms of the disease) does not enable one to identify the causative agent.

The relationships between microbes and disease are further complicated by variations in one's response to infection by a virus. The same microbe can sometimes cause entirely different sets of symptoms in different individuals. Typhoid Mary was a carrier of typhoid, but she was far from being unique in her resistance to the disease; her notoriety came about because she insisted on continuing her work as a cook after being informed that she was a threat to others. Other carriers of typhoid existed. In fact, there is substantial variation between individuals in terms of their resistance to every known disease-causing microbe. Some people resist infection better than others, and some infected individuals exhibit symptoms that are more or less severe than others infected with the same type of microbe.

Because different microbes may produce the same symptoms, and because the same microbe may produce different symptoms in different individuals, diagnosis involves art as well as science. Symptoms alone are often not enough to indicate the type of microbe responsible. This is not to deny the role of cause and effect. There are still causes and there are still effects, but in medicine the link between the two is not always transparent. Of course, one might argue that if more information was available—if diagnosticians could grow cultures of microbes that they believed responsible for a particular patient's symptoms and if they had access to more information on each individual's ability to resist specific infections—then it might be possible to talk more convincingly about the laws of cause and effect in relation to the identification of disease. Though this is true, as a practical matter that type of information is usually not available. Even in the case of the common cold, it is difficult under the best of circumstances to tell when someone is infected with a coronavirus, simply because such viruses are hard to grow in a laboratory environment. Nor is there any convenient way to obtain detailed information about a patient's ability to resist specific microbes even if the microbes themselves are known beforehand. Diagnosis remains an inexact science.

As a consequence, physicians rely (knowingly or unknowingly) on a statistical approach to diagnosis. The physician takes measurements (temperature, blood pressure, heart rate, etc.) and questions the patient about the onset of symptoms, the presence or absence of pain, and other factors. These measurements and questions serve to sharpen the diagnosis by eliminating (or at least reducing the likelihood) that certain microbes are responsible for the patient's condition. Given an unfamiliar set of symptoms, this statistical approach requires the physician to have an encyclopedic knowledge of diseases and their causes, but the idea is relatively easy to understand. One continues to answer ever more specific questions until a "most likely" diagnosis is obtained. Computers have been used with some success to diagnose diseases via this approach. The computer begins by requesting input—each input

This spore of the fungus *Blastomyces dermatitides* can cause a condition similar to the flu. In areas where it is endemic, it causes one or two cases per 100,000 people. Under such conditions, it is easy to misdiagnose. (Courtesy of Dr. Leanor Haley, Centers for Disease Control and Prevention)

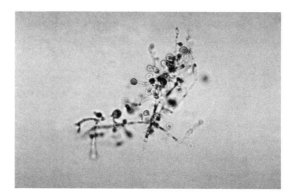

giving rise to another request—until the computer's most likely diagnosis is obtained.

Lack of information and the complex relationships that exist between symptoms and the microbes that cause them are not the only difficulties that prevent a doctor from obtaining an accurate diagnosis; there is also the matter of time. A sick patient needs a diagnosis in order to begin a course of treatment. It is in theory possible for a physician to continue gathering information indefinitely in the hopes of obtaining an ever more accurate diagnosis. Under these circumstances, of course, the patient will either recover without treatment or die. Physicians who require certainty prior to acting are of little help to their patients.

The complex relationships that exist between microbes and the symptoms they cause (and the limited time that physicians have to unravel the link between them) have historically made for some very interesting and challenging situations.

Treating the Symptoms

As described in the preceding section, it is sometimes the case that physicians are required to diagnose a disease and prescribe a course of treatment even though they have only the most modest insights into the cause of the symptoms that they seek to cure. Consequently, they reason statistically. They must continue to reason statistically after they have arrived at their diagnosis and have begun their course of treatment. They seek correlations between the actions they take and changes in the condition of the patient. The strengths and weaknesses of this type of reasoning are best illustrated in the first successful attempt to treat cholera.

Cholera first found its way onto the island of Great Britain during the second pandemic (1826–37). The germ theory of disease had not yet been proposed, and there was a great deal of speculation about the cause of the new disease. Recall that cholera is a dramatic and often deadly disease: Symptoms include violent diarrhea and vomiting; dark circles form about the eyes; the skin becomes corrugated; breathing is labored. But these exterior symptoms suggested no method of treatment to physicians during the Second Pandemic. To learn more about the effects of the disease, they performed autopsies. Their autopsies revealed that the walls of the intestines were covered with a pasty material; the blood had become very viscous and dark, and sometimes the lungs had collapsed. One physician, William O'Shaughnessy, thought to test the blood of cholera patients and discovered that their blood had a much lower proportion of water and salt than the blood of people without the disease. This observation caused O'Shaughnessy to propose injecting a saline solution back into the veins of the cholera patients. He published his novel idea in 1831 in the British medical journal *Lancet*, but he seems never to have followed through on his own suggestion. He wrote that further research into the effects that the injected salts would have on the blood should be undertaken before the procedure was attempted.

Not long after O'Shaughnessy's article was published, Thomas Latta, a Scottish doctor, read it. There was a great deal that Latta did not know about cholera, and it is doubtful that he understood O'Shaughnessy's procedure better than O'Shaughnessy himself. Latta did not understand the cause of cholera; he did not know how fast to inject the solution, he did not know what to put into the solution, and he was unclear about when the treatment should be stopped. But people dying from cholera surrounded him.

Latta's first patient to receive the novel treatment was an elderly woman who had not responded to what he described as "the usual remedies." (It is not known what these entailed.) She was close to death when, over the course of 30 minutes, Latta injected six pints (almost 3 L) of solution into one of her veins. Her color returned, her breathing was no longer labored, and she regained consciousness. She seemed to have recovered. Exhausted, Latta left her in the care of the hospital surgeon and went to rest. The symptoms of cholera returned, but the surgeon did not alert Latta. In less than six hours, the patient died.

Latta had discovered the technique called rehydration, the first successful treatment for cholera. He went on to apply his treatment to other cholera patients. The results were promising. There were, of course, failures. Keep in mind that neither Latta's equipment nor his solution was sterilized, and that his implementation of the idea could not have been cruder. Nevertheless, the method was an enormous improvement over the treatments of his contemporaries, which sometimes involved bleeding the patients with leeches, administering laxatives or tobacco enemas, or even attaching patients to batteries. Despite his successes and his creativity, Latta's discovery had little impact on the practices of his contemporaries. Latta died before most other physicians recognized his contribution. Understanding the reasons that Latta's contemporaries failed to appreciate his discovery, which he published in the medical journal *Lancet* in 1832, helps us

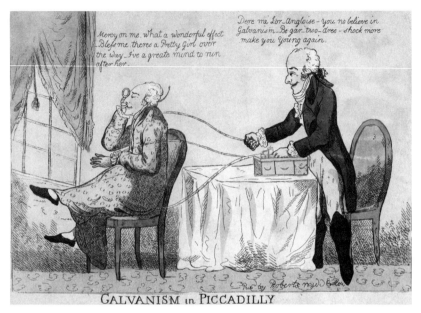

GALVANISM in PICCADILLY

This picture, which dates to about 1800, satirizes the then-popular medical practice of attempting to cure disease by connecting patients to batteries. [SSPL/The Image Works]

appreciate the difficulties of placing too much emphasis on symptoms rather than causes.

Whether or not people are treated for cholera, some recover. Cholera bacteria vary in their virulence, and humans vary in their ability to resist the effects of the germ. In fact, no matter what the physicians of the time did to their patients, there were always some who recovered from both the treatment and the disease. Physicians already knew some patients would live and others would die. What they wanted to know was the relationship between their treatments and the survival of their patients. That some of Latta's patients survived being injected with a saline solution does not by itself mean that rehydration therapy cured them, any more than those cholera survivors who were treated with leeches owed their survival to the leeches rather than their own hearty constitutions. Every doctor had his (and they were mostly male physicians in this time and place) own favorite method of treatment, and each doctor tended to attribute the survival of individual patients to his own treatment methods and the skill with which the treatment was administered. Medical journal articles of the time were largely anecdotal—physicians enjoyed describing their favorite methods of treatment and the ensuing individual successes.

Today researchers expend a great deal of effort attempting to ensure that what happened to Thomas Latta does not happen again. Sophisticated methods of comparing medicines and treatment protocols have evolved in an effort to identify which medicines and which protocols work and which do not. Demonstrating that one method of treatment is better than another requires that one try the method on a large population and compute average survival rates while taking into account the age and initial conditions of the patients as well as a variety of other factors. These computations are then compared with other statistical surveys of other groups of patients who were subjected to other treatment regimens to determine which methods are the most effective. This statistical method of treating disease attempts to find a treatment regimen that will do the greatest good for the greatest number, but it takes little account of isolated cases. It is the best method available today, but it is far from perfect. It emphasizes effects rather than causes, symptoms rather than the organisms responsible.

The Notion of Cure

For most of human history there were no cures for diseases. To be sure, people were treated for their illnesses. There have always been physicians of one sort or another, but the treatments were generally ineffective because the microbes that caused the diseases were unaffected by the treatments. Whenever a disease began to work its way through a population, there were only three possible outcomes for each person in the group: An individual would escape infection, survive infection, or die. This bred a remarkable stoicism on the part of many. In a letter to his wife Sofia, Thomas Gallaudet, a prominent American educator of the first half of the 19th century, wrote that the two of them (he and Sophia) had to remain prepared for the possibility that their children could die at any time. He was right. It was not unusual for parents to bury at least some of their children.

More than two centuries ago, Edward Jenner's smallpox vaccine was an extremely important innovation in the struggle against disease-causing microbes. But vaccination is a preventive measure. It does little for those already ill.

About a century ago, researchers learned how to create a fourth outcome for the sick: People could be cured of their diseases in the sense that the actions undertaken by their physicians resulted in the destruction of the microbes with which they were infected. In 1910, Salvarsan, a drug that successfully cured syphilis, was first successfully tested. Sulfa drugs were developed in the 1930s. (Most types of sulfa drugs are no longer therapeutically beneficial because sulfa-resistant bacteria have become commonplace.) Penicillin was first available for general use in the 1940s. Streptomycin followed penicillin. It was created in 1943 and was the first drug effective against tuberculosis. Other lesser-known but important antibiotics followed: cephalosporin (an alternative antibiotic for those sensitive to penicillin) was first synthesized in the 1940s. Erythromycin (useful in treating certain strains of pneumonia as well as Legionnaire's disease) and vancomycin (often characterized as the antibiotic of last resort because it is so effective), two other important antibiotics, were created in the 1950s. All of these medicines remain in use.

They also have two other characteristics in common: First, although each of these drugs was initially highly effective against certain types of bacteria, drug-resistant strains have evolved for each. Second, these are antibiotics, that is, no matter how effective they are against certain types of bacteria, none of them is effective against viruses. With the help of these antibiotics, individuals infected with certain strains of bacteria were (and are) cured. The causes of their dis-

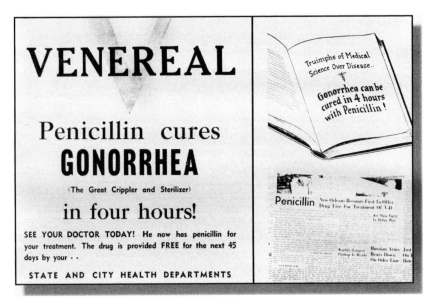

This early poster promotes penicillin as a "wonder drug." It shows no awareness of the dangers of the indiscriminant use of the drug. [Courtesy of Centers for Disease Control and Prevention]

"Prevention of Consumption" railway sign from 1930s England. The first effective treatment of consumption—better known today as tuberculosis—was not available until 1947. Spitting helped spread the disease. [NRM/SSPL/The Image Works]

eases are eliminated. But in the process of curing the sick, the drugs themselves have become increasingly less effective because they have given rise to drug-resistant strains of the very bacteria they were created to destroy. (See chapter 13 for a discussion of this phenomenon.)

Scientists have had less success in curing viral infections. The first antiviral drug, amantadine, was introduced in 1966. Most antiviral drugs are much newer, and their effectiveness against viruses does not rival the effectiveness of their antibacterial counterparts. Neuraminidase inhibitors, for example, a class of drugs used to treat influenza, have been shown to lessen the severity of symptoms and to shorten the duration of the disease by an average of only one day, provided the five-day course of treatment is begun within 48 hours of the onset of symptoms. These kinds of results are typical. Most antiviral drugs are only modestly effective.

It is also typical of many antiviral drugs that they do not cure the disease in the sense that antibiotics cure bacterial infections. The best-known example of the way that drugs help manage rather than cure a disease is the current class of drugs used to treat HIV/AIDS. These drugs, administered together in carefully regulated doses, control the virus that causes AIDS. One measure of their success is called the viral load test, a blood test that measures the number of viruses per milliliter of the patient's blood. Individuals with a high viral load—with viruses occuring in densities of 100,000 or even 1 million viruses per milliliter—tend to develop AIDS quickly and live only a short time. Those with a low viral load—say 1,000 copies of the pathogen per milliliter—generally live longer. The drugs used to control HIV often have a dramatic effect on the viral load. They sometimes even lower the viral load to a level at which the virus is no longer detectable. But this is not a cure. If the patient discontinues the drug regime, the viral load begins to increase. Therefore, even when the virus can no longer be detected via the viral load test, it must still be true that individual pathogens are present in the body. AIDS drugs save lives; they make it possible to live with the pathogen. But unlike antibiotics, which destroy the pathogen responsible for the disease, AIDS drugs merely bring the responsible pathogen under control by reducing its numbers.

As in the case of the antibiotics, there is now evidence that certain strains of HIV have evolved to become resistant to some drugs that were previously effective in controlling it. (At the time of this writing, there is no evidence that the viruses for which the neuraminidase inhibitors were created have developed resistance to those drugs, but it is only a matter of time before resistant strains are discovered.) As with their antibiotic counterparts, it is the *act* of using the antivirals on a genetically heterogeneous population of viruses that causes resistant strains to evolve.

This is a unique time in history: Individuals infected with a variety of pathogens can be cured; others can manage deadly diseases indefinitely with the help of new classes of drugs. While many of us have lived our entire lives in the age of the "wonder drugs" and so take their existence for granted, we should not forget that there are still individuals among us who remember what life was like before penicillin. It was a dangerous time. (Penicillin was originally tested on a man who was dying from an infection he acquired when he cut himself shaving.) There is currently no reason to be complacent. The balance between the new drugs and the pathogens they were created to destroy is a delicate one, and many diseases have so far proved impossible to cure. Whether these—usually viral—diseases will prove to be curable in the short term is an open question. Equally uncertain is whether science can evolve as fast as the microbes it seeks to destroy.

THE ECOLOGY OF MICROBES

Disease microbes may be understood on the molecular level (chapter 14); they may be identified and studied in terms of the symptoms they cause (chapter 15); they can also be studied as part of a larger ecosystem. Scientists who study microbes on this third, macro level are often interested in how microbes move from host to host and even region to region. They also seek to identify those environments that microbes inhabit when they are not infecting humans. Finally, they sometimes develop plans to alter the environment in order to control the spread of disease. Plans to alter the environment—and this may entail either the human or nonhuman environment—may be simple or complex, highly invasive or barely noticeable. Past recommendations have included such noninvasive procedures as installing screens in the windows of houses. More aggressive approaches to saving lives have included draining large wetlands (used effectively to control malaria) or the relocation of entire villages.

This approach first saw real success in the 19th century with the work of the early epidemiologists John Snow and Henry Whitehead, who showed that contaminated water was a principal means of cholera transmission. In more recent years, the study of the transmission patterns of pathogens and their role in the larger environment has attracted the attention of ecologists as well as epidemiologists. Sometimes understanding the relationships that exist between microorganisms and the larger environment is the only way that one can establish effective control procedures.

This ecology-based approach to understanding disease-causing microbes sometimes depends on information about the microscopic structure of the pathogens or their effect on humans; often it does not. Snow's theory about the transmission mechanism of cholera, for example, was formulated before the germ theory of disease was even discovered. In this sense, many of the insights obtained in this branch of science are better understood as ecological in nature because they depend upon insights into relationships *between* the microbes and their environments rather than on a detailed understanding of either.

It must be kept in mind that a microbe's environment can be as "large" as a river valley (this is true, for example, of the microbe responsible for the disease onchocerciasis, or river blindness, a leading cause of blindness worldwide), or it might be as "small" as an air-conditioning unit (for example, Legionnaires' disease). Because of the size of these microbes, both river valleys and air-conditioners are more than large enough to accommodate entire, richly populated micro-ecosystems. Identifying these ecosystems and understanding their properties are some of the challenges scientists face when they study the ecology of microbes.

Patterns of Transmission

When investigating a disease, researchers are confronted with a usually incomplete list of sick individuals. As additional information is gathered, researchers collect more names as well as personal information, which may include each individual's address, age, and sex. Depending on the nature of the disease, they may also collect information on each individual's diet, daily activities, location of the individual's home in relation to water, the presence or absence of screens on the individual's home, health history, family history, presence of family pets, or any number of other factors. The questions they ask depend on what they suspect the cause of the illness to be. What the researchers want is a common factor, something that many of the affected individuals have in common. The common factor may or may not enable them to discover how the microbe responsible for the disease is transmitted, but the identification of such factors is generally considered a step in the right direction.

This book has already recounted, for example, how Legionnaires' disease was discovered: All of the infected individuals had been in the same hotel, and that hotel was cooled by an air-conditioning system that circulated the microbe through the air. The fact that they had all visited the same hotel at the same time was the clue. Some clues are harder to discover. Suppose that the common factor shared by members of a group of people sharing a common disease was that they had been bitten by an infected mosquito, fly, or other insect. This factor is much harder to identify because the infected individuals would usually be unaware that an infected insect had bitten them and thus would be unable to point to a shared experience. Furthermore, they and most other individuals in the same community would presumably have been bitten many times previously by uninfected insects.

Identifying transmission patterns is further complicated by the complexity of the ecology of microorganisms. Biologists sometimes talk about *niches*, habitats sufficient to supply an organism with what it needs to live. For example, woodpeckers eat insects living under the bark of trees and from tree hollows. This is their niche. Other birds occupy other niches; they do not generally have the necessary beak structure to obtain insects in the way that the woodpecker does. They are adapted to other niches. In the absence of woodpeckers, some other organism will eventually evolve to occupy the niche usually occupied by woodpeckers, because the niche exists even if the woodpeckers are not there to exploit it. For example, in the Galápagos Islands, there are no woodpeckers, but a type of finch, first described by Charles Darwin, has learned to use twigs and cactus spikes to remove insects from the hollows of woody plants so that they can be eaten. The finches occupy a niche that would otherwise be occupied by woodpeckers. Presumably, if there were woodpeckers on the Galápagos Islands, they would displace the so-called woodpecker finches because they are better adapted to this niche.

What distinguishes the study of the ecology of microorganisms from that of their larger counterparts is that the number of niches available for microorganisms is enormous. Pathogens are so small that they can live inside other organisms as well as alongside them. Some microbes have adapted to live in the gut of small insects. Others live in standing water. Still others live in the soil, on our skin, and even inside other microorganisms. (The organism responsible for cholera, for example, has been observed living inside an amoeba, another, larger microorganism.) Identifying transmission patterns generally involves discovering something about the niches occupied by the microorganism of interest, and this can be very difficult to do, in part because they can be so difficult to find.

Consider the problem of the distribution of cholera. Occasionally, individuals in widely separated areas of the world contract cholera from contaminated seafood. The cholera germ has been found in oysters in Florida and fish in Queensland, Australia. Cholera cases have been linked to the consumption of raw or slightly cooked seafood in Singapore, Guam, Louisiana, and Portugal. Scientists suspect that a more widespread outbreak in Peru in 1991 was linked with seafood consumption, although this has not been proved. To discover the way that cholera microbes could infect sea life in areas where the cholera germ was not thought to be present was a difficult research problem. First, researchers had to identify these often very small disease clusters (the cases are often isolated in time and in space) and then discover that the cholera germ could live inside certain species of sea life. This hardly solves the problem, however, since initially cholera was not known to be endemic to some of the areas where the individuals contracted the disease. How, the researchers wanted to know, did the cholera germ infect the shellfish?

The answer lies in world shipping practices. A ship that is not loaded with cargo floats high in the water. With the center of gravity high above the water's surface, the ship is harder to handle in rough seas. When a ship leaves port empty—perhaps, for example, it has just unloaded its cargo and is preparing to embark for another port—it needs to fill its ballast tanks, large tanks inside the ship designed to hold water, lower the ship's center of gravity, and make the ship easier to handle. This is done by simply pumping water out of the harbor and into the tanks. When the ship arrives at the next port where it will load new cargo, it simply pumps the water out of the tanks and back into the ocean. What researchers discovered is that when the ships pumped water out of the relatively shallow harbor, they were loading not just water but micro-ecosystems filled with microorganisms. (These are sometimes called microhabitats.) The organisms survived in the ballast tanks of the ships until the ship's tanks were pumped out, at which time the ship deposited the microhabitats into some distant harbor. When the researchers analyzed the contents of the ballast tanks in an attempt to prove their hypothesis, they found the microbe responsible for cholera along with many other types of microbes. The chain was now clear: from areas where cholera is endemic, to the ballast tanks of ships, to new ports of call, to shellfish, to the infected individual. Such complex and unexpected routes of transmission are more the rule rather than the exception.

Because the niches inhabited by microorganisms are so diverse, every attempt to determine how disease-causing organisms are transmitted to humans depends on new insights and often new investigative techniques. The discoveries about transmission patterns that result from these investigations are usually unique to the case at hand. Once researchers have identified the transmission patterns of one disease-causing organism, and once they have made the necessary recommendations for protecting the public health, they begin to study a different organism with entirely different habitat requirements and entirely different modes of transmission. By contrast, in the study of the genetics of microorganisms, it is generally true that the same techniques used to sequence the genome of one organism will sequence the genome of another.

Despite the difficulties involved, the investigation of the transmission patterns of various microbes is one of the most important ways of protecting the public health, because discoveries in this area can lead to large-scale changes in human behavior that can prevent the transmission of disease. It is important to realize that our health-care system is fragile. It works well only when the number of sick people is not too large. No national health-care system has the capacity to cope with a nation of sick people. Insights into the microhabitats of disease-causing microbes enable public-health authorities to create policies that reduce the probability of widespread disease.

Microbes in the Environment

There are far more microbes in a handful of fertile soil than there are humans on Earth. While microbes are often described as simple organisms—simple in structure, that is, when compared to higher organisms—their microhabitats can be very complex. Not only are there often many microorganisms in a small volume of space, but also they show wide variation in structure. How these microorganisms are related to one another and how their microhabitats affect the larger environment is usually not clear. The ecology of microorganisms is a field that is still in its infancy. No one is even sure what sorts of organisms exist: It is estimated that no more than a few percent of all microorganisms have been classified. The best that can be done here is to indicate some of the complexity that exists in their habitats and life cycles by examining two commonly occurring pathogens. (Control methods for these pathogens are described in the next section.)

One class of pathogens with a complex life cycle that is also a major threat to world health is the class of microorganisms responsible for the disease *schistosomiasis*. This disease, which infects approximately

200 million people, is often described as only second to malaria as the world's most serious parasitic infection. Schistosomiasis is caused by any one of five species of flatworms. These creatures are also known as

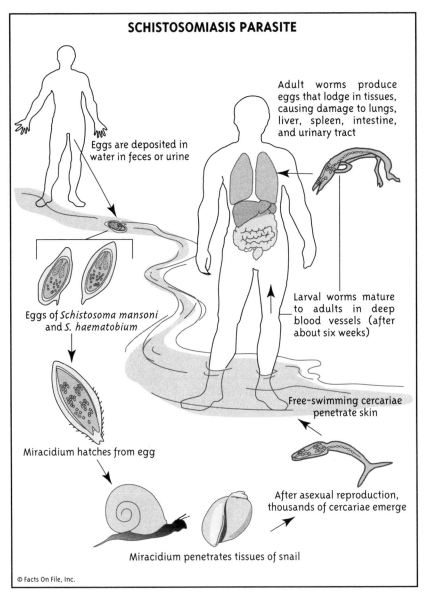

SCHISTOSOMIASIS PARASITE

Adult worms produce eggs that lodge in tissues, causing damage to lungs, liver, spleen, intestine, and urinary tract

Eggs are deposited in water in feces or urine

Eggs of *Schistosoma mansoni* and *S. haematobium*

Larval worms mature to adults in deep blood vessels (after about six weeks)

Miracidium hatches from egg

Free-swimming cercariae penetrate skin

After asexual reproduction, thousands of cercariae emerge

Miracidium penetrates tissues of snail

© Facts On File, Inc.

The life cycle of the schistosomiasis parasite

Two boys wading in a stream despite the warning sign on the bank, "Danger—There Is Bilharzia." (*Bilharzia* is another term for schistosomiasis.) [Courtesy of Centers for Disease Control and Prevention]

blood flukes and as schistosomes. The ancient Egyptians knew the disease, but the cause was not identified until 1851 by the German scientist Theodor Bilharz. (Schistosomiasis is also called bilharzia.)

The disease begins when someone comes into contact with water contaminated with a form of the schistosoma parasite called cercariae. These tiny creatures are able to penetrate the skin in a few seconds. Once inside, the parasite works its way into a blood vessel, where it grows into a long male or female worm. This generally occurs within 45 days after it first infects its host. The worms reside in male/female pairs. Depending on the type of schistosomiasis-causing microbe, most of the worms live either in blood vessels of the bladder or in blood vessels that line the intestine. Once they have found their permanent home, the female will lay anywhere from a few hundred to a few thousand eggs per day, depending on the species. This goes on for years.

The worms themselves damage the organs in which they reside and about half the eggs remain in the body, where they become lodged in other organs and are the cause of additional injury. Because the worms are often ubiquitous, individuals are generally infected repeatedly, with

disease: Brain damage, learning disabilities, nervous system damage, and deafness are all associated with the disease.

Meningococcal disease is contagious, but it is not easily contagious. The bacteria are transmitted via droplets in the air from sneezing or coughing and can also be transmitted by kissing or by sharing eating utensils or cups and glasses. They are generally only transmitted through prolonged, close contact—the type of living conditions one finds in dormitories, for example. Outbreaks generally occur in small clusters and are more common in winter and spring.

As a feature of our environment, *N. meningitidis* is noteworthy because it does not survive long outside humans. There are no known animal reservoirs. It does, however, infect large numbers of humans. In fact, many of us are carriers of this disease, meaning we are infected with the bacteria that cause meningococcal disease but show no symptoms. Estimates of the percentage of the population infected with the bacteria range from 5 to 25 percent, depending on the region under consideration. The great majority of these individuals are asymptomatic carriers; they are not ill and never become ill. Essentially, our bodies *are* the environment for *N. meningitidis* because it is generally not found outside a human body. Why some people become ill while the great majority of individuals remain healthy is not known. (Methods of control for this disease are discussed in the next section.)

Controlling Microbes by Controlling Their Environment

Controlling disease-causing microbes has sometimes proven to be quite difficult. To be sure, there have been some remarkable successes. Smallpox was eliminated from the environment and only survives in research laboratories. Cholera, once found in virtually every country on the planet, has been largely brought under control. (Unlike smallpox, cholera exists outside of the human body and so is much more difficult to eliminate as a health threat.) Despite these and several other successes—for example, yellow fever, polio, and measles—there are a number of microbes that have proven very difficult to eliminate or even control. Their resilience can, in some cases, be explained by the relationship of the disease-causing microbes to their environment. Disrupting that relationship is the key to controlling the disease. In this section, we examine control efforts for the two diseases described in the preceding section, schistosomiasis and meningococcal disease.

There are many places that are perfect environments for the parasites responsible for the disease schistosomiasis. The parasites thrive when there is plenty of water, plenty of people, and plenty of the aquatic snails upon which they depend. The people who live in these areas are often poor and have no access to supplies of safe water. Instead, they are surrounded by contaminated water. They do, however, have the same needs as those of us who have access to safe water supplies. They need to wash themselves and their clothes; they need water to cook and to drink. They have no choice but to come into daily contact with water that is rife with the parasite that is often so injurious to their health. Furthermore, it is important to understand that even if they obtain safe water supplies, they live in an environment that is—from a public-health point of view—still quite dangerous. Agriculture is extremely important in these areas. Most people farm, and farmers have no option but to work in the fields. Children will still play in the water. There is a large segment of the population that even under the best of circumstances will become infected, reinfected, and reinfected again. A safe water supply is an important step, but control efforts cannot stop there.

In order to adequately address the problem of continued reinfection, health authorities have attempted to attack the parasite directly by manipulating the environment in which it lives. Because the parasite spends so little time outside the body of a host, either human or snail, control efforts have been directed at manipulating these two microenvironments.

Safe, cheap, and effective drugs have been developed to treat schistosomiasis. In a certain sense, these drugs work by making the body of the human host as toxic as possible to the parasite. In this sense, they are successful, but they, too, are of limited value when used alone. The problem (again) is that once cured, the individual may be quickly reinfected. The main benefit of the drugs is that they reduce the risks associated with long-term, continuous exposure to the parasites; they arrest the disease in its early stages, but they do nothing to prevent reinfection.

A second line of attack has so far not proved successful: a schistosomiasis vaccine. If the immune system could be "taught" to destroy the parasite whenever it entered the body, this would solve the problem of continual reinfection for most individuals—and make a tremendous difference to the lives of the many millions of individuals who live in areas where the schistosomiasis parasite is endemic.

A third line of attack is to destroy the "intermediate" host, the snail. The life cycle of the schistosomiasis parasite *requires* it to infect a snail after it is excreted from the human body and before it infects another human. To this end, various poisons called molluscicides—poisons specific to mollusks—have been developed. These, too, have had some effect in reducing rates of the disease, but by themselves they have yet to produce the desired result: complete control of the parasite. Part of the problem is that it is difficult to treat every micro-habitat inhabited by the snails, and one infected snail will produce many thousands of individual parasites. Any untreated body of water will quickly fill with cercariae, the form of the parasite that infects humans.

A fourth line of attack is to implement better sanitation. There is a brief period of time after the egg of the parasite is excreted by the human and before it infects the snail during which it is exposed to the environment. Better sanitation could interrupt the life cycle of the parasite at this stage of development by preventing transmission to the snail. It should be kept in mind, however, that the level of sanitation with which most readers of this book are familiar has not been attained in much of the world. It is extremely expensive to implement, and while it is technically feasible, the countries most affected tend to be financially less able to afford to implement the necessary technologies. Additionally, it should be remembered that those most affected are often farmers, and the sanitary standards required to disrupt the life cycle of the parasite are, in practice, often not met even among farm workers in developed countries such as the United States.

Progress in controlling schistosomiasis has been slow. The microbes responsible for the disease have proven to be resistant to all efforts to control them. It remains a serious health threat to hundreds of millions of people in large regions of the world.

In contrast to the pathogens responsible for schistosomiasis, the bacteria responsible for meningococcal disease are found almost exclusively in the human body. There are no nonhuman reservoirs for the disease, and since they can be transferred directly from one individual to the next via kissing, for example, they can spread without ever exposing themselves to the outer environment. Control efforts, there-fore, must concentrate on those who are infected because infected indi-viduals are virtually the only environment inhabited by *Neisseria meningitidis*, the microbe that is one of the principal causes of the dis-ease. (Although there are other pathogens responsible for the disease, this is the only causative microbe that will be considered here.)

As stated in the previous section, *N. meningitidis* generally infects individuals without causing any symptoms, and a large number of individuals are carriers of the disease. Efforts at controlling the disease center on two approaches: quick diagnoses and treatment of symptomatic individuals and vaccination.

Because the disease progresses so quickly, it is imperative that it be quickly diagnosed and treated. There are many antibiotics that are effective—several strains of *N. meningitidis* exist, and all are susceptible to a range of antibiotics. The procedure recommended by the World Health Organization (WHO) is to admit the patient immediately to a hospital if infection is suspected, diagnose the disease, and, if the results are positive, begin treatment with antibiotics immediately. (They suggest diagnosis first and treatment second because if treatment is begun before the diagnosis is complete, the antibiotics may make it difficult to confirm the presence of the bacteria and so make it difficult to determine if the right treatment regimen was undertaken.)

Vaccination is, then, the only preventive option available, but opinions on how vaccination programs should be implemented vary. Saudi Arabia, for example, immunizes its entire population. Many other countries do not. The effects of vaccines in this case are complex, and the question of whether or not to vaccinate an entire population is a matter of debate.

The idea behind mass vaccination programs is to create what is called herd immunity—to make so many people immune that the microbes responsible for the disease have no easy path to move from one vulnerable individual to the next. (A vaccination is rarely 100 percent effective, and every vaccination program will miss at least a few individuals, so there are always some individuals in the population that are still vulnerable.) But not all vaccinations are created equal. Vaccinations for strains of *N. meningitidis* responsible for meningococcal disease tend to be of limited duration. Vaccinations also tend to be of limited effectiveness in very young children, a high-risk group for the disease in any case. Consequently, attempting to keep enough of the population immunized to obtain herd immunity is problematic and requires a lot in the way of public-health resources.

WHO, instead, recommends that in the event of an outbreak, all close contacts of the infected individual be inoculated, and, because there is a delay between the time one is vaccinated and the time an immune response is obtained, that all close contacts take antibiotics for two weeks after vaccination. If there is a large-scale outbreak of meningococcal disease—and there is a region of Africa called the

African Meningitis Belt, where such epidemics have occurred—WHO recommends that everyone in a district where there is a large-scale outbreak be vaccinated as well as those in surrounding districts.

In the United States, it has long been known that college freshmen are at higher risk for meningococcal disease than the general population. Many colleges now recommend that students residing in on-campus housing be vaccinated against meningococcal disease, and the state of Maryland requires the vaccine for this segment of the population.

These strategies cannot eliminate the microbes responsible for meningococcal disease. While the disease can be very dangerous, the fact that it occurs at low frequencies, that many infected individuals are asymptomatic, and that the current vaccines are of limited duration mean that there is no strategy currently available to eliminate this disease from the environment where it resides, the human body.

The examples described in this section show that it is sometimes very difficult to bring a dangerous disease under control. While the human immune system is exquisitely adapted to resisting pathogens, we live in a virtual sea of them. Advances in technology have made it possible to augment the immune response and effectively resist a variety of diseases that were once responsible for large numbers of deaths. But ever-increasing public expectations about the ability of microbiologists, physicians, and epidemiologists to protect the public health from pathogens, as well as the extraordinary ability of pathogens to adapt to control measures, ensures that there will be no quick victory over disease. There is still a great deal to be done.

GLOSSARY

anthrax An infectious disease caused by the spores of a bacterium. Symptoms may include lesions on the skin or lungs.

antibiotic An agent used to destroy microorganisms or inhibit their growth; not useful against viruses.

antibody Proteins that bind to antigens that enable the body to destroy microbial invaders.

antigen Protein on the surface of a cell or virus that stimulates the production of antibodies.

antiviral Type of medicine used to destroy or inhibit the reproduction of viruses.

aseptic The absence of pathogens, e.g. an aseptic laboratory.

bacterium (plural **bacteria**) Single-celled microorganism.

biohazard Pathogen or biological condition that poses a threat to humans.

biological warfare Warfare that uses pathogens as weapons.

biosafety Safety with respect to research on living organisms.

bioterrorism The use of microorganisms to harm or coerce.

Centers for Disease Control and Prevention (CDC) Centers for the study of infectious diseases located in the United States.

cholera Virulent diarrheal disease caused by the bacterium *Vibrio cholerae*.

DNA (deoxyribonucleic acid) The molecule of heredity for all living organisms and most viruses.

endemic To belong to a particular region.

epidemic An outbreak of a (usually infectious) disease that affects a large proportion of a particular population.

epidemiology The study of the transmission and control of disease in populations.

gene chip A device to determine the function of particular genes

genetic engineering   Branch of science concerned with the direct intervention into genetic processes, often involving the insertion of genes into an organism's genome.

genotype   The collection of genes belonging to an organism.

germ   A microorganism.

hemorrhagic fever   Any of a group of viral diseases characterized by the quick onset of symptoms including shock and heavy bleeding.

immune system   The entire bodily system whose function it is to protect the body from foreign bodies.

infectious disease   Any contagious disease.

influenza   A highly contagious viral disease with symptoms commonly associated with the flu, such as fever, aches, and stuffiness. The viruses that cause influenza belong to a particular "family" called Orthomyxoviridae.

latency period   The period of time between infection and the appearance of symptoms.

malaria   A disease caused by parasites of the genus *Plasmodium* that is transmitted by the bite of the anopheles mosquito.

meningitis   An infection of the fluid that surrounds the brain and spinal cord and inflammation of the meninges, membranes that surround the brain and spinal cord.

meningococcal disease   Meningitis.

microbe   Microorganism.

microbiologist   One who studies that branch of biology concerned with microorganisms.

mutate   A change; in genetics, it refers to random permanent changes in DNA.

niche   A habitat in the larger environment in which an organism can live.

pandemic   An epidemic that covers a very wide geographical area.

parasite   An organism that exploits a host in order to live, with resulting injury to the host.

pathogen   The cause of a disease.

penicillin   An antibiotic originally produced from molds of the genus *Penicillium*.

phenotype   The physical properties of an organism. The phenotype is the result of interaction between the genotype and the environment.

plague   The disease caused by the bacterium *Yersinia pestis*. The word *plague* is sometimes also used to refer to any virulent, contagious disease.

polio (also called **poliomyelitis**)   A viral disease that affects the muscles and can lead to permanent paralysis.

protozoan A member of a very broad, loosely defined class of microorganisms that can be found virtually everywhere and contains many of the most virulent human diseases.

quarantine The practice of isolating a person, animal, or plant from its surroundings in order to isolate the disease the creature carries; also, the practice of isolating the organism until it can be determined whether the creature is carrying the disease of interest.

SARS (severe acute respiratory syndrome) Respiratory illness caused by a coronavirus.

schistosomiasis A disease caused by a parasitic worm that, left untreated, can cause permanent injury.

selection pressure A cause of differential reproductive success that may lead to changes in the gene frequencies present within a species.

spirilla Spiral-shaped, stiff-bodied bacteria.

spirochete Spiral-shaped, flexible bacteria.

spore A unicellular body produced by some plants and microorganisms.

streptomycin A common antibiotic, once famous for its effectiveness against tuberculosis.

sulfa drug A member of a class of bacteria-inhibiting chemicals.

syphilis A venereal disease caused by the bacterium *Treponema pallidum.*

tuberculosis A highly contagious disease caused by the bacterium *Mycobacterium tuberculosis.*

typhoid (also called **typhoid fever**) A contagious disease caused by *Salmonella typhi.*

vaccine A substance—such as a suspension of live or dead microorganisms—used to induce the immune response.

vector Any organism that transmits a pathogen.

vibrio A genus of comma- or S-shaped bacteria.

virus A large class of nonliving microorganisms that can only reproduce in living cells.

weaponize To make into a weapon; used with respect to microorganisms.

West Nile virus The virus responsible for causing West Nile disease.

World Health Organization (WHO) The United Nations organization responsible for monitoring and protecting the public health.

yellow fever Viral disease transmitted by the bite of an infected mosquito.

Yersinia pestis Bacterium responsible for the plague.

FURTHER READING

The History of Disease

Microbes are a purely biological phenomenon, but their effects are not. To understand some of the effects microbes have had on societies and some of the effects that societies have had on microbes, read about the history of disease.

Cook, Noble David. *Born to Die: Disease and New World Conquest, 1492–1650.* Cambridge: Cambridge University Press, 1998. This scholarly work consists of a relentless description of the devastation caused by newly introduced diseases as long-separated cultures mixed and clashed for the first time. It is a topic that receives more attention each year.

Giblin, James Cross. *When Plague Strikes: The Black Death, Smallpox, AIDS.* New York: Harpercollins, 1995. A very accessible account of some of the deadliest diseases in history and society's response.

Jones, James H. *Bad Blood: The Tuskegee Syphilis Experiment.* New York: Free Press, 1993. Medicine has never been purely about science, and diseases have rarely affected all classes of society equally. This is the story of one of the most notorious "medical" experiments in American history.

Kolata, Gina. *Flu: The Story of the Great Influenza Pandemic of 1918 and the Search for the Virus That Caused It.* New York: Farrar, Straus, and Giroux, 1999. With a new and very virulent strain of avian flu in Asia currently threatening to make the transition to humans, this story is more important than at any time since 1918.

Morris, R. J. *Cholera 1832: The Social Response to an Epidemic.* New York: Holmes and Meier Publishers, 1976. This scholarly work is full of eyewitness accounts of the 1832 cholera epidemic. It shows clearly how disease affects society and how society affects the transmission of disease.

Oldstone, Michael. *Viruses, Plagues, and History.* Oxford: Oxford University Press, 1998. More stories of some of the most dangerous diseases in history.

Rau, Weldon Willis. *Surviving the Oregon Trail, 1852.* Pullman: Washington State University Press, 2001. By horse and wagon, large numbers of settlers and miners traveled along the Oregon Trail. Many of them died—most of those as a result of disease, especially cholera. This book, which is not principally about diseases or microbes, nevertheless conveys some sense of how vulnerable the people of this time were to pathogens.

Williams, Greer. *Virus Hunters*. New York: Alfred A. Knopf, 1959. There are still copies of this excellent old book to be found. The sections on history are quite good; much of the rest, of course, is out of date. It is worth reading, however, in part because it effectively conveys the tremendous optimism about the ability of science to defeat disease that was part of this field for so long—until researchers developed an appreciation for how adaptable viruses could be.

The Science of Microbes and the Science of Disease

Microbiology and epidemiology are two important sciences associated with the study of disease-causing organisms, but practicing scientists are determined to find answers rather than stay in any one discipline.

Crawford, Dorothy H. *The Invisible Enemy: A Natural History of Viruses*. Oxford: Oxford University Press, 2000. A sometimes breathless but fact-filled description of viruses and their effects, including a chapter devoted to the relationships that exist between viruses and cancers.

Goodsmit, Jaap. *Viral Sex: The Nature of AIDS*. Oxford: Oxford University Press, 1997. Written for a general audience by a specialist in AIDS research, this book contains many interesting stories of researchers struggling to gain insight into the HIV virus. One chapter contains a fascinating account of an attempt to find HIV-like viruses in ancient Egyptian mummies.

Levy, Stewart B. *The Antibiotic Paradox: How the Misuse of Antibiotics Destroys Their Curative Powers*. Cambridge, Mass.: Perseus Publishing, 2002. The more antibiotics are used, the less effective they become. Misuse accelerates this phenomenon. This overly long book examines in detail how this is occurring, but it spends much less time asking why antibiotics are so frequently abused than it does describing their misuse.

Spielman, Andrew, and Michael D'Antonio. *Mosquito: A Natural History of Our Most Persistent and Deadly Foe*. New York: Hyperion, 2001. A comprehensive history of the sickness and death inflicted by mosquitoes and humanity's sometimes successful attempts to protect itself. Fascinating reading.

Tabak, John. *Probability and Statistics: The Science of Uncertainty*. New York: Facts On File, 2004. This book contains specific information about the way mathematics and statistics have been applied to the study of disease.

Personal Perspectives on Disease

Diseases affect individuals as well as societies. Here are two interesting first-person narratives about how diseases have affected lives.

Kehret, Peg. *Small Steps: The Year I Got Polio.* Morton Grove, Ill.: Albert Whit-
    man and Company, 1996. A very accessible and affecting account of the
    author's experience with poliomyelitis.
McCormick, Joseph B., Susan Fisher-Hoch, and Leslie Alan Horvitz. *Level 4:
    Virus Hunters of the CDC.* Atlanta: Turner Publishing, 1996. A personal tale
    of what is involved in the study of some of nature's most deadly microbes.

WORLD WIDE WEB SITES

There are a great many sites on the Web devoted to discussions of diseases, the microbes that cause them, and related subjects, but only some of these are scientifically or historically accurate. The following sites contain additional information about some of the topics covered in this book.

General Information Sites

Perhaps the two best Web-based sources of information about pathogens and the diseases they cause are maintained by the Centers for Disease Control and Prevention (CDC; www.cdc.gov) in Atlanta, Georgia, and the United Nation's World Health Organization (WHO; www.who.int). Both these sites contain enormous amounts of information about specific diseases, how they are transmitted, and the medicines that are used to control them. Much of the information is technical; some of it is aimed at a general audience. The CDC Web site is somewhat more comprehensive and a little easier to navigate, but the WHO Web site has a more international feel.

History of Disease

Billings, Molly. "The Influenze Pandemic of 1918." Available online. URL: http://www.stanford.edu/group/virus/uda. Accessed June 20, 2005. This is a thoughtful, well-written account of the influenza pandemic of 1918.

Foëx, B. A. "How the Cholera Epidemic of 1831 Resulted in a New Technique for Fluid Resuscitation." *Emergency Medicine Journal* 20 (2003). Available online. URL: http://emj.bmjjournals.com/cgi/content/full/20/4/316.

Accessed June 21, 2005. This article contains a thorough account of Thomas Latta and his treatment of cholera.

Frerichs, Ralph R. John Snow Web page. Department of Epidemiology, University of California at Los Angeles. Available online. URL: http://www.ph.ucla.edu/epi/snow.html. Accessed June 21, 2005. Contains an excellent account of John Snow, the Broadstreet cholera epidemic, and numerous related articles, including Snow's own article on cholera.

Thucydides. "The History of the Peloponnesian War." Translated by Richard Crawley. The Internet Classics Archive. Available online. URL: http://classics.mit.edu. Accessed June 21, 2005. This site contains a very affecting account of the plague that struck Athens by one who witnessed it.

Vainio, Jari, and Felicity Cutts. "Yellow Fever." Available online. URL: http://www.who.int/vaccines-documents/DocsPDF/www9842.pdf. Accessed June 21, 2005. This is a carefully researched and extensive history of yellow fever, written for experts. A more user-friendly version of the same paper can be found at a site maintained by McGill University in Montreal, Canada. Available online: URL: http://sprojects.mmi.mcgill.ca/tropmed/disease/yellowfev/history.htm. Accessed June 21, 2005.

Germ Warfare/Bioterrorism

Centers for Disease Control and Prevention. "Emergency Preparedness and Response." Available online. URL: http://www.bt.cdc.gov/agent/agentlist. asp. The CDC Web site has numerous links and articles about pathogens that might be employed in an attack, along with descriptions of their properties.

Flight, Colette. "Silent Weapon: Smallpox and Biological Warfare" British Broadcasting Corporation. Available online. URL: http://www.bbc.co.uk/history/war/coldwar/pox_weapon_01.shtml. Accessed June 21, 2005. To read how smallpox has been used as a weapon of war in previous centuries and how countries prepared to use it during the cold war, see this report prepared for the British Broadcasting Company.

Frerichs, Ralph R. Epidemiologic Information on Bioterrorism Web page. Department of Epidemiology, University of California at Los Angeles. Available online. URL: http://www.ph.ucla.edu/epi/bioter/bioterrorism. html. Accessed June 21, 2005. This site contains reprints of a variety of articles on bioterrorism (including the 2001 anthrax attack), commentaries, and stories about preparedness.

Genetics

American Society of Microbiology. "Genetic Tools and Techniques." Available online. URL: http://www.microbeworld.org/htm/aboutmicro/tools/genetic.htm. Accessed June 21, 2005. For a very accessible account of the concepts and technologies associated with gene sequencing, see the site maintained by the American Society of Microbiology.

Genoscope. Genoscope homepage. Available online. URL: http://www.
genoscope.cns.fr. Accessed June 21, 2005. Genoscope is the name of the
French National Sequencing Center. It contains numerous articles about
the genetics of humans, mosquitoes, and various other organisms.

Evolution and Drug Resistance

Iseman, Michael D. "Evolution of Drug-resistant Tuberculosis: A Tale of Two
Species." National Academy of Sciences. Available online. URL:
http://www.pnas.org/cgi/reprint/91/7/2428. Accessed June 21, 2005. This
is a readable and highly informative paper about a very important subject.
WGBH Educational Foundation. "What Can We Do to Reduce Antibiotic
Resistance?" Available online. URL: http://www.pbs.org/wgbh/evolution/
survival/enemy/statement_04.html. Accessed June 21, 2005. This Web
page contains statements by four experts on a difficult problem.

Diseases of Special Concern Today

Centers for Disease Control and Prevention. "Avian Influenza (Bird Flu)."
Available online. URL: http://www.cdc.gov/flu/avian. Accessed June 21,
2005. Avian influenza is one of the most urgent of all public-health threats
because of its potential to turn into a global pandemic.
Centers for Disease Control and Prevention. "CDC Plague Home Page."
Available online. URL: http://www.cdc.gov/ncidod/dvbid/plague. Accessed
June 21, 2005. This site is an excellent source of information about the
plague. Especially interesting is information about how scientists now
understand the health risks posed by the Black Death.
World Health Organization. "Department of Communicable Disease Surveil-
lance and Response Home Page." Available online. URL: http://www.who.
int/csr/disease/en. Accessed June 21, 2005. This site contains a list of 15
dangerous diseases and what scientists, health-care workers, and government officials are doing to bring them under control.

INDEX

Note: *Italic* page numbers indicate illustrations.

A

Abel, Niels Hendrik 49
accidents 103–111
acquired immunity 145
acquired
  immunodeficiency
  syndrome. *See*
  HIV/AIDS
acute otitis media
  (AOM) 125–128, *126*
Aedes albopictus 35
Africa
  Ebola in 115
  HIV/AIDS in
    36–37, *37*, 120,
    121
  Marburg virus in
    116
  meningitis in *165*,
    169–170
  monkeypox in 4
  polio in 58
  West Nile virus in
    34
African green monkey,
  Marburg virus in
  115–116
African trypanosomiasis
  78
agriculture, and spread
  of disease 14, *15*
AIDS. *See* HIV/AIDS
airplanes, quarantine of
  98
alveoli 117

amantadine 155
American Legion
  58–60. *See also*
  Legionnaires' disease
animals. *See also* specific
  animals
  influenza in 17
  malaria in 50
  monkeypox in 4
  plague in 43
  West Nile virus in
    35
Anopheles aegypti 34
Anopheles mosquitos 50
Antelope (Oregon) 92
anthrax
  in biological war-
    fare 33, 89,
    90–91
  death from 33
  inhalation form of
    33
  in letter attacks
    (2001) 3, *32*,
    32–34, 93
  treatment of 33–34
antibiotics
  for acute otitis
    media 125–128
  for anthrax 33–34
  as cure 31, 154–155
  discovery of 31,
    80, 154
  and gene frequen-
    cies 130

for Legionnaires'
  disease 58
for meningitis 165,
  169
from molds 9, 80
and perception of
  disease 31
for plague 43
resistance to. *See*
  drug resistance
for tuberculosis 49,
  80
antibodies 116, 145
antibody surveys 116
antigens 145
antiviral drugs 155–156
AOM. *See* acute otitis
  media
apes, SIV in 120
Aristotle (Greek
  philosopher) 74
arsenic, for syphilis
  78–79
arthritis 78
aseptic surgery 77
Australia, mousepox in
  109–110
autopsies 150–151
avian influenza
  epidemic of
    (2003–2004) 98,
    99–100
  in humans 98, 100,
    142